MW00478470

gestalten

The MONOCLE
Travel Guide Series

Milan

All rights reserved. No part of this publication may be reproduced or transmitted in any form or by any means, electronic or mechanical, including photocopy or any storage and retrieval system, without permission in writing from the publisher.

Respect copyrights, encourage creativity!

For more information, please visit *gestalten.com*

Bibliographic information published by the Deutsche Nationalbibliothek: The Deutsche Nationalbibliothek lists this publication in the Deutsche Nationalbibliografie; detailed bibliographic data are available online at *dnb.d-nb.de*

MIX
Paper from
responsible sources
FSC® C011712
www.fsc.org

This book was printed on paper certified by the FSC®

Monocle editor in chief and chairman: *Tyler Brûlé*
Monocle editor: *Andrew Tuck*
Books editor: *Joe Pickard*

Designed by *Monocle*
Proofreading by *Monocle*
Typeset in *Plantin & Helvetica*

Printed by *Offsetdruckerei Grammlich, Pliezhausen*

Made in Germany

Published by *Gestalten*, Berlin 2017
ISBN 978-3-89955-923-1

© Die Gestalten Verlag GmbH & Co. KG, Berlin 2017

Welcome
—— Get familiar

If the Italian cities are a family – and really they are, banded together from independent states in 1871 – Milan is the *enigmatic* middle child: she wears sunglasses at the dinner table and dropped out of her MBA to go to fashion school. She may have garnered a reputation for being a little industrial and uptight compared to her southern siblings but scratch beneath the surface and you'll find a dynamic, *forward-thinking* and eminently liveable city.

Milan's location in the shadow of the Alps – closer to Zürich, Innsbruck and Munich than Rome – has lent the city a fluid character: centuries of *intermingling* are apparent throughout the city's architecture, dialect and even work ethic. In bleaker periods this proximity to the rest of Europe led to foreign nations such as the Spanish and Austrians occupying the city but, having thrown off these shackles, the sense of *pride* is like a fever among its people.

Perhaps it's this hard-fought liberty that has driven the Milanese to *impress* and *excel*. Since the 1950s the city has been the hub of Italy's booming *fashion* industry and the country's financial centre; thanks to the Salone del Mobile it has also established itself as the unrivalled *design capital* of the world.

But Milan can be a closed book. There's more to this city than the *dazzling Duomo* though you'll need to know where to look: that foreboding palazzo may well contain a verdant courtyard, a world-class tailor or even a rooftop bar. Allow us to reveal the chicest boutiques, the most cutting-edge galleries and the restaurants serving the silkiest *risotto Milanese*. Sunglasses at the dinner table? *Ma certo.* — (M)

Contents
—— Navigating the city

Use the key below to help navigate the guide section by section.

 Hotels

F **Food and drink**

R **Retail**

T **Things we'd buy**

E **Essays**

C **Culture**

D **Design and architecture**

L **Lake escapes**

S **Sport and fitness**

W **Walks**

Map
—— The city at a glance

Unusually for a European city, Milan has no river or coastline to anchor it: instead, everything revolves around the mighty Duomo. Seen from above, the city resembles a series of concentric ripples, with the gothic cathedral at its epicentre.

Clustered around this focal point are historical Brera, the old artists' quarter; fashionable Quadrilatero della Moda, packed with luxury boutiques; and ancient Sant'Ambrogio. These are bound by the city's former gates, including the Porta Ticinese and Porta Romana.

But Milan has grown both upwards and outwards in recent years and beyond the old centre are up-and-coming neighbourhoods that boast a certain gritty charm: Isola in the north is an increasingly popular haunt for the city's night owls. Meanwhile, glittering skyscrapers by big-hitters such as Zaha Hadid are transforming the skyline around Porta Nuova and CityLife.

Milan certainly breaks with the traditional Italian cityscape of terracotta rooftops and classical crenellations – and it does so brilliantly.

Pirelli HangarBicocca

ISOLA

LORETO

o Monumentale

NUMENTALE

Bosco Verticale

Stazione Centrale

CENTRALE

Corso Venezia

CITTÀ STUDI

Fondazione
Giangiacomo Feltrinelli

PORTA
GARIBALDI

PORTA NUOVA

PORTA VENEZIA

mpione

Giardini Pubblici

Pinacoteca di Brera

BRERA

QUADRILATERO
DELLA MODA

RISORGIMENTO

ello
esco

Teatro alla Scala

Villa Necchi Campiglio

DUOMO

Galleria Vittorio Emanuele II

CORDUSIO

SAN BABILA

MONFORTE

QUE VIE

Duomo

PORTA VITTORIA

ROBIO

MISSORI

Linate Airport

GUASTALLA

olonne di
n Lorenzo

Torre Velasca

TICINESE

PORTA ROMANA

Porta Ticinese

CALVAIRATE

BOCCONI

Università Bocconi

0   500M   N

Fondazione Prada   RIPAMONTI

Need to know
—— Get to grips with the basics

How long to linger in a restaurant, where to catch the cool crowd when fashion and design weeks descend, which football team to cheer for and when to hit the shops. Our top tips and quick facts will make moseying around Milan that bit more rewarding.

Restaurant advice
Take your time

Italian waitstaff will never hurry you away from your table, no matter how in demand it may be. Enjoy the last sips of your espresso and ask for *il conto* (the bill) at your leisure. Or go straight to the register, where you'll be paying anyway. Most restaurants will add a small *coperto* (cover) or *pane* (bread) charge. Waitstaff earn a living wage so are not expecting tips but a particularly good meal or server merits a sign of appreciation – usually up to 10 per cent of the bill, in cash only. For a coffee bar or lunch spot, be sure to order at the register first and then give your receipt to the person behind the counter to receive your order; here, always be prepared to pay in cash.

Aperitivo
The pre-dinner ritual

A longtime Milan tradition, aperitivo means that even the most modest bar wouldn't dream of serving a glass of bubbly without a few peanuts, crisps or olives. Some bars have developed elaborate buffets where students and cost-conscious revellers turn cheese and couscous platters into dinner, while the more chic and restaurant-oriented areas use aperitivo as an introduction to their kitchen. Leave room for dinner and stay on the lighter side of alcohol: the idea of aperitivo is to open your appetite. As the Italians say, "*La fame vien mangiando*" (hunger comes with eating). We've tested out the best spots, all in the name of research of course (*see page 42*).

Oh go on then, just one more negroni...

Weather
Capricious climes

Visitors often assume that Milan is blessed with the same clement climate as Tuscany. Sadly not. The city's northern position doesn't preclude Mediterranean heat but it does come with its fair share of rain and icy blasts. July is both the hottest month – with the mercury regularly climbing above 30c – and the wettest. Meanwhile, in January the temperature can drop to below zero. But don't lock yourself indoors, pack some good boots and your chicest mac: Milan in the rain has a charm of its own.

Etiquette
Politeness rules

The Milanese appreciate a "*buongiorno*" or "*buona sera*" when entering a shop or building. Don't forget your "*per favore*" and "*grazie*" when dealing with the manner-conscious locals and don't be surprised if a word or two quickly gets you into an extended conversation with a stranger. They're not as cold as their reputation would have you believe.

Coffee
Counter culture

In Milan, as in any Italian city, coffee culture follows a set of golden rules. Most cafés have two sections: the coffee-and-pastry counter and the grave-looking cashier. Never ask for the bill at the former; you'll doubtless be ignored. Milky coffees such as cappuccinos and lattes (side note: flat whites are hard to come by here) are traditionally consumed before noon, while espresso can be taken at all times of day. For a truly Italian coffee break, add a *cornetto* (croissant) to the ticket.

Pollution
Emission admission

While the Milanese adore outdoor revelry as much as their southern counterparts, the landlocked valley city suffers from a persistent pollution problem that – at its worst in winter – cloaks the city in a milky grey haze, surpassing the EU's acceptable levels and forcing emergency traffic shutdowns. In summer, if the smog and sweltering heat become overbearing, do as the locals do and hightail it to the beach or nearby Lago di Como.

ight, can eryone see the uomo now?

Designer city
Good crowd

Several times a year, the hordes descend on Milan to soak up its high style and design. April's Salone del Mobile is a huge design event, with every nook and exhibition space promoting the future of furniture. Hundreds of thousands flock to the citywide events – and most of them end up at Bar Basso after 22.00. Meanwhile, the fashion weeks (men's in January and June, women's in February and September) flood Milan with a more self-consciously styled set.

So does this make it a dogwalk?

Inside knowledge
Above and beyond

Much of Milan's action is concealed behind closed doors. Approach the city with an insider attitude and you'll find that many of its best shops, studios, galleries and gardens are hidden from the street, located in elegant courtyards or up a flight of stairs or two. Take the chance to peer in when a door is open; if you're lucky a native friend (or guidebook) will help you out. Take note: the buzzer labels may not always be self-explanatory. If in doubt, ask the *custode* (porter).

Opening hours
Mind the gap

You may find it strange that a world-class city can close for lunch but Milan, for all its cosmopolitan airs, is still very much an Italian town. As anyone here will tell you, "*Il pranzo è sacro*" (lunch is sacred). Don't go anywhere between 12:30 and 15:30 without checking whether they'll be open first; ditto for all day Sunday and even Saturday afternoons and Monday mornings. With so much dedication to rest and meal times, restaurants stick to a rigorous schedule: arrive before 15.00 if you want to eat lunch and plan to sit down for dinner between 19.00 and 22.00. If hunger calls between meals, there's always gelato.

Football
Back of the net

While many Milanese remain tied to the Catholic church, Saturdays and Sundays are devoted to another calling: fervidly rooting for either AC or Inter Milan, both hometown football teams and among the best in Italy. Locals pick a team for life, forever looking down on the other team and its *tifosi* (supporters). From August to May, weekend games are played at the San Siro stadium, where high-spirited crowds that can number up to 80,000 pack the stands. Once owned by major Italian businessmen (AC Milan by Silvio Berlusconi and Inter by oil magnate Massimo Moratti), both teams were recently sold to Chinese investors. Passions remain as high as ever.

Hotels
—— At home in the city

There was a time when most of the hospitality options that Milan had to offer were stately – if a little stuck-up – old-world hotels. Today, however, plenty of smaller boutique stop-ins have sprung up, each sporting a peculiarly Milanese character and a quiet modesty that reveals its charm from within.

While the majority of establishments are located to the northeast of the city centre, a stone's throw from the retailers of the Quadrilatero della Moda, many have taken to newly revamped (or simply rediscovered) neighbourhoods, putting the claim that Milan is only good for shopping well and truly to bed.

One thing that hasn't changed is the focus on impeccable interiors: expect designer decor and the highest-quality furnishings. This is a city that's used to hosting the world's fashion and design elite, so you'll have no trouble finding somewhere to catch up on your beauty sleep.

①
Maison Borella, Navigli
The quiet life

Unassuming and discreet, this hotel overlooking the canal is an intimate 30-room affair – and surprisingly quiet, considering its location in buzzy Navigli. Four years of sensitive restoration were needed to revamp the 19th-century *casa di ringhiera*, a typical Milanese house with a shared balcony. The result, finished in 2011, is all the more tasteful thanks to the vintage furnishings chosen by collector Raimondo Garau (*see page 51*).

The main part of the hotel wraps around an internal courtyard and each floor's railings are covered in sweetly scented jasmine. Under a coffered ceiling on the ground floor, Ristorante Bugandè serves chef Davide Brovelli's contemporary versions of Lombard classics, including the omnipresent *cotoletta* (veal cutlet) and creamy risotto.
8 Alzaia Naviglio Grande, 20144
+39 02 5810 9114
hotelmaisonborella.com

MONOCLE COMMENT: For extra privacy opt for the Maison Privée, a nearby outbuilding that houses just seven rooms.

Hotel Viu, Sarpi
Top of the world

This hotel pays homage to a
recent addition to the skyline:
Bosco Verticale (*see page 104*). The
124-room property sports vertical
gardens on two sides of its exterior,
with an assortment of flora such
as jasmine, ivy and wisteria.

The interiors have been given
a subdued lick of paint and feature
a tasteful mix of sandstone, oak
and marble. Gio Ponti armchairs
sit in the lobby, while pieces from
Italian brand Molteni&C are
found throughout the rooms. For
commanding views of the Alps,
head to the top-floor breakfast
area with its adjacent rooftop
pool. Chef Giancarlo Morelli's
formal restaurant at ground level
serves a sophisticated Lombard-
centric menu.
6 Via Aristotile Fioravanti, 20154
+ 39 02 8001 0910
hotelviumilan.com

MONOCLE COMMENT: The rooftop
space is the focal point here. As
well as being a great place for
brunch, you can also request a
sunrise yoga lesson.

③

Park Hyatt, Duomo
Banking on it

Few other options marry tranquillity with such a grand, central location: Park Hyatt is just a few steps from the spires of the Duomo and opposite the Galleria Vittorio Emanuele II. Inside this former bank headquarters, which was built in 1870, 106 rooms are decorated in a minimal, Asian-inspired style. Each features an Italian touch – be it Murano-glass wall lights, a Venetian stucco or room perfume devised by Turin-based Laura Tonatto – and travertine marble abounds, especially in the bathrooms where you'll often find the minibar (one of the hotel's quirks).

Breakfast is served under the airy glass dome, while Mio Bar offers bites and excellent cocktails – including 12 variants of a Bloody Mary. If you order just one thing, make it a club sandwich, arguably the world's best.

1 Via Tommaso Grossi, 20121
+39 02 8821 1234
milan.park.hyatt.com

MONOCLE COMMENT: It's worth upgrading your room to a suite: book the Duomo Suite for an outdoor Jacuzzi with a view.

④
Senato Hotel, Porta Venezia
Home from home

Discerning business travellers
and holidaymakers flock to the
43-room Senato Hotel for its
enviable location between the
Giardini Pubblici and the fashion
boutiques on Via della Spiga.
The former residence of a family
of Milanese industrialists, the
five-floor neoclassical property
was tastefully remodelled by local
architect Alessandro Bianchi,
who designed every element of
the makeover, from light fixtures
to furniture.

Bedrooms come with oak
parquet flooring, while bathrooms
feature wall-to-wall grey-white
Carrara marble. The understated
public spaces – all of which are
kitted out with custom furnishings,
such as hand-worked brass lighting
– include a peaceful patio used
for all-day drinking and dining.
Lombard influences dominate the
menu and the bar serves prized
bubbly from Franciacorta.
22 Via Senato, 20121
+39 02 781 236
senatohotelmilano.it

MONOCLE COMMENT: Do as the
locals do and head to the plant-
filled rooftop terrace to relax.

Three classics

Before the recent crop of smaller boutique hotels appeared in Milan, the hospitality scene was dominated by the grandeur of old-world hotels. Here's our selection of the places that show off the best of traditional Italian elegance.

01 Baglioni Hotel Carlton, Quadrilatero della Moda: Some rooms have modern updates but the hotel's best are the ones that feature beautiful antique furniture. Opt for the Montenapoleone terrace suite for full-on glamour.
baglionihotels.com

02 Petit Palais, Ticinese: Opened in 2007 with an extensive and meticulous renovation, this 17th-century building has the chandeliers, silk tapestries and ornate bedframes of a historical mansion.
petitpalais.it

03 Grand Hotel et de Milan, Quadrilatero della Moda: Located on busy Via Manzoni, this stalwart of Milan's hospitality scene has been here since 1863. It was home to composer Giuseppe Verdi for 27 years, hence the name of its restaurant: Don Carlos.
grandhoteletdemilan.it

Small wonder
———

Alongside a busy shop, modern restaurant, garden café and art gallery, the complex at 10 Corso Como features a small hotel. Its name – 3 Rooms – gives a good indication of size and exclusivity.
3rooms-10corsocomo.com

⑤
Palazzo Segreti, Cordusio
Designer deco

Tucked away on a quiet lane between the Duomo and Castello Sforzesco, the 18-room Palazzo Segreti is the perfect base from which to explore the city.

Inside the 19th-century palazzo, the owners have given each room its own identity by making the most of furniture from Italy's big design brands. Cappellini beds, Kartell and Moroso side tables and chairs, plus lighting by Artemide and Flos mix beautifully with exposed brick walls and hardwood floors. Those eager to sojourn longer should seek out the hotel's separate block of luxury apartments next to Porta Garibaldi (*see below*).
8 Via San Tomaso, 20121
+ 39 02 4952 9250
palazzosegreti.com

Le Suite dreams

Palazzo Segreti operates seven serviced apartments in the newly developed district of Porta Nuova. All suites have different interior designs but for a grand view of the spike of the UniCredit Tower, book yourself into the Attico.
palazzosegreti.com

⑥
TownHouse Duomo, Duomo
Room with a view

The small TownHouse Hotels chain occupies two of Milan's most coveted spaces. The 58-room TownHouse Galleria may sit inside the Galleria Vittorio Emanuele II itself but it's this little sibling that steals the spotlight with its magnificent view: TownHouse Duomo is the only luxury hotel directly overlooking the cathedral.

The latter's 14 suites were conceived by eight different designers and all but two enjoy floor-to-ceiling windows looking onto the fabled vista. Some, such as the futuristic Swan Room, are an acquired taste but most are the perfect marriage of superlative products and cleverly considered design. Suite 11, which was designed by Massimo Magaldi, is noteworthy for its furniture by Riva 1920, Fiorito marble and mid-century style.
2 Via Silvio Pellico, 20121
+ 39 02 4539 7600
duomo.townhousehotels.com

MONOCLE COMMENT: Dinner at chef Felice Lo Basso's in-house Michelin-starred restaurant is a must: the Puglian delivers his native cuisine without pomp.

⑦
Room Mate Giulia, Duomo
Grand designs

Oviedo-born, Milan-based designer Patricia Urquiola was tasked with creating the interiors for this centrally located palazzo. Consequently the 85 rooms feature bold colours, unstuffy layouts and furniture courtesy of Cassina.

Communal areas are filled with Urquiola's designs for Moroso, Glas Italia and Kettal, while the pink-marble floors and terracotta bricks reflect the Lombard style. Hanging on the walls are Milanese artist Sandro Fabbri's Matisse-like watercolours (also available to buy) and more art by local creatives is spread across the six floors.
4 Via Silvio Pellico, 20121
+39 02 8088 8900
room-matehotels.com

MONOCLE COMMENT: If you're partial to a lie-in, this is the place for you: mattresses are super comfy and breakfast is served until noon.

CasaBase, Tortona
It's all about that base

CasaBase inhabits a converted
factory in the creative district
of Tortona. Its 10 rooms are
midway between hotel and artists'
residence, hosting creative types
working on projects at the cultural
centre Base downstairs as well as
regular visitors – whatever their
budget (bunk-bed and shared-
room options are available).

Bright doubles are furnished
with pieces by Vitra, as well as
vintage 1950s and 1960s gems.
But CasaBase's strongest suit
is its communal space: cosying
up on colourful modernist
armchairs, you're likely to strike
up a conversation with other
guests – perhaps over breakfast,
delivered from Un Posto a Base,
the skewers-only restaurant on-
site. If you want to tinker away
on your laptop, there's also a co-
working space.
34 Via Bergognone, 20144
base.milano.it/casabase

Touch base
————

The large venue below
CasaBase hosts more than
400 events a year, including
workshops, music shows,
exhibitions and film screenings.
There are also special
programmes during the
design and fashion weeks.
base.milano.it

Three hotel restaurants

For those in search of fine
dining, a series of top chefs
have taken over some of the
city's hospitality hallmarks.

01 Seta at Mandarin
Oriental, Quadrilatero
della Moda: Two-Michelin-
starred chef Antonio Guida
brings years of experience
and his Puglian tradition.
mandarinoriental.com

02 Vun at Park Hyatt,
Duomo: Chef Andrea
Aprea's Neapolitan
background shines
through in the varied menu.
milan.park.hyatt.com

03 La Veranda at Four
Seasons, Quadrilatero
della Moda: Dinner
gets serious in this airy
glasshouse, with chef Vito
Mollica's classy dishes.
fourseasons.com/milan

Four Seasons, Quadrilatero
della Moda
Old discoveries

At the centre of this hotel in the
heart of the fashion district is the
cloister of a 15th-century convent.
When the Four Seasons renovated
the three buildings that make
up the hotel in 1987, details of the
original structure were unearthed
and made use of: now ancient
granite columns and frescoes can
be spotted in the lobby and lounge.
The best of the 118 rooms overlook
the peaceful inner garden but those
with a view onto prime shopping
street Via Gesù are equally quiet;
try the Caruso suite, created in
collaboration with the menswear
brand – a neighbour.

For one of the hotel's highlights,
head underground: set in what
used to be the wine cellar is a spa
designed by Patricia Urquiola that
features an atmospheric brick-
vaulted pool and warm, wood-clad
treatment rooms.
6-8 Via Gesù, 20121
+ 39 02 77 088
fourseasons.com/milan

MONOCLE COMMENT: Two Pierre-
Yves Rochon-designed suites have
a different feel to the rest of the
hotel; book the Fashion suite for a
mid-century-inspired atmosphere.

10

Bulgari Hotel, Brera
Serene stay

Hidden at the end of a private alley, this hotel and its relaxed outdoor bar are a quiet pocket in the bustle of Brera; the fact that it backs onto the area's botanical gardens (*see page 135*) adds to the serene atmosphere. Designer Antonio Citterio created the stark monochrome façade, as well as a moody hall and restaurant filled with his own furniture designs for Flexform and Maxalto.

The 58 rooms are a brighter affair. Clad in light-oak panelling and pastel fabrics, most have teak balconies that open up onto the hotel garden; in spring, the smell of camelia, magnolia and wisteria below is a pleasant addition to an alfresco breakfast. With plenty of sunlight flooding its mosaic-tiled indoor pool, the spa is a lesson in how to make the most of underground space and includes a wonderfully secluded Jacuzzi.
7B Via Privata Fratelli Gabba, 20121
+39 02 805 8051
bulgarihotels.com

MONOCLE COMMENT: The garden is the perfect location for an afternoon aperitivo.

Food and drink
—— Stepping up to the plate

The Milanese may be habitually in a hurry but when it comes to drinking and dining they know how to slow things down a notch or two. The day unfailingly begins with the requisite coffee stop while evening is heralded with a well-appointed aperitivo before dinner, which can last into the early hours.

The spirit of true Milanese food remains unchanged: the cooking is slow, the dishes rich and unpretentious. And naturally, Italy's fashion capital knows how to make food look good on a plate.

Since Expo 2015, Milan has boasted one of the most exciting food scenes in Italy, with everything from bustling bistros to elevated street food and gourmet pizza. And the same goes for booze: the birthplace of Campari, Fernet Branca and Amaro Ramazzotti is now home to Italy's first artisanal gin distillery. *Buon appetito e salute.*

Restaurants
Table talk

 ①

A Santa Lucia, San Babila
Understated glamour

Opened in 1929 by Leone Legnani and his wife Rosetta as a pizzeria-cum-restaurant near the Duomo, A Santa Lucia moved to its current location in San Babila in 1957. Jacketed waiters move briskly, presided over by black-and-white photos of cinema's golden-age stars such as Frank Sinatra and Liza Minnelli and the stream of intellectuals, entrepreneurs and musicians who have graced the restaurant over the years.

The fare is Neapolitan but beyond the exemplary pizzas there's a mean steak on offer. Under the ownership of Alberto Cortesi the understated charm of this Milanese institution hasn't changed: it's still the quintessential *vecchio ristorante chic.*
3 Via San Pietro all'Orto, 20121
+39 02 7602 3155
asantalucia.it

2

Erba Brusca, Conca Fallata
Grown in the garden

Set on a bucolic canal on the outskirts of the city (read: a decent taxi ride), Erba Brusca is run by French-US chef Alice Delcourt (*pictured*), whose previous positions include a stint at The River Café in London.

A mainstay of the menu is the pasta with clams, truffles and wild *erba brusca* (sorrel). As with many of the ingredients that end up in her colourful dishes, the sorrel is plucked directly from the adjoining garden: come in the warmer months when the tables spill out onto the patio. Delcourt's partner – sommelier and maître d' Danilo Ingannamorte – will help you navigate the natural wine list.
286 Alzaia Naviglio Pavese, 20142
+39 02 8738 0711
erbabrusca.it

Rural retreat
———
Greenery envelopes the sun-dappled terrace

Street eats
———
01 Luini
Pizza dough, stuffed and fried.
luini.it
02 Giannasi
Take-away roast chicken.
giannasi1967.it
03 Ravioleria Sarpi
Beef, pork and vegetarian dumplings.
+39 331 887 0596

⑤ Langosteria Bistrot, Porta Genova
Catch of the day

Milan may be some 150km from the nearest stretch of coast but the city's seafood offering can be exceptional and Enrico Buonocore's Langosteria often secures the cream of the catch. The Milan-born restaurateur opened his first site in Tortona in 2007, followed by this bistro in 2012 (a third venue inside the Excelsior Mall followed in 2016). This is the most intimate of the bunch.

Expect Catalan-style king crab, an impressive oyster selection, carpaccio and tempura. Sit at the bar to watch the chefs in action.
2 Via Privata Bobbio, 20144
+39 02 5810 7802
langosteria.com

④ Giacomo Bistrot, Risorgimento
In the club

With its dark wood panelling, gilded mirrors and moody lighting, Giacomo Bistrot's interiors – designed by Studio Peregalli – have a touch of the gentlemen's club about them. As befits such surroundings, we suggest you linger at the fin-de-siècle bar with a bellini before heading to your table.

The bistro, which serves a rich menu focusing on meats and foie gras, is part of a mini empire built by Tuscan Giacomo Bulleri that comprises restaurants, a coffee shop, a *pasticceria* and his own take on the traditional *tabaccheria*.
6 Via Pasquale Sottocorno, 20129
+39 02 7602 2653
giacomobistrot.com

③ Casa Ramen, Isola
Oodles of noodles

Inspired by New York's Ippudo, Luca Catalfamo opened this pint-sized ramen restaurant (one of Milan's first) in hip Isola in 2013. Finding similarities between the Japanese staple and that of his native Italy, Catalfamo decided to use durum wheat flour – traditionally used to make pasta – for his noodles. His rigorous approach and original take scored him an invitation to open his own space in Tokyo's Shin-Yokohama Ramen Museum, the first non-Japanese to do so. The braised pork-belly dish is the crowd-pleaser.
25 Via Porro Lambertenghi, 20159
+39 02 3944 4560
casa-ramen.it

6
Dry, Porta Garibaldi
Upper crust

This smart restaurant, co-owned by chef Andrea Berton, kick-started the city's gourmet pizza movement when it opened in 2013. Simone Lombardi's offering, whipped out of the Neapolitan brick-fired oven, is arguably still the best in the city. You can't go wrong with the *pizze classiche* but the bite-sized focaccia laced with *vitello tonnato* (a heady veal-and-tuna combo) is textbook. Be sure to leave room for a cocktail: we recommend the French 75.

Dry is only open in the evening; for lunch head to the newer sister venue Dry 2, near Porta Venezia.
33 Via Solferino, 20121
+ 39 02 6379 3414
drymilano.it

Pizza

While it may not have the same pizza heritage as Italian cities further south, Milan now boasts a suite of venues serving pizza to rival that found in Naples or Rome thanks to a new wave of chefs who are mixing creative methods with respect for tradition.

The key is in the dough – and, more specifically, the flour that's mixed into it – which typically uses an extra-long fermentation process for maximum flavour and lightness. Ovens have improved (they're often custom-made in Naples) and while the archetypal margherita is still the benchmark against which a *pizzaiolo*'s skills can be measured, there are countless options when it comes to toppings.

01 Lievità, Wagner:
pizzeria-lievita.com
02 Marghe, Porta Vittoria:
marghepizza.com
03 Berberè, Isola:
berberepizza.it
04 Olio a Crudo, Tortona:
+39 02 4537 5930

Blank canvas
———
Understated interiors let the food and drink shine

Must-try

Cotoletta alla Milanese from Trattoria del Nuovo Macello, Calvairate

According to tradition, the perfect *cotoletta* is a bone-in -veal loin chop that's been aged for two weeks and then dusted in flour, dipped in beaten eggs, breaded and fried in butter. This is one of the best in town.
trattoriadelnuovomacello.it

⑦
Tokyo Table, Porta Genova
Japan's finest

Tokyo Table's first Italian venture opened in 2017 and soon became the city's go-to place for *otsumami*: tapas-style snacks with a mix of either meat, fish or vegetables.

The space is bright and airy, with whitewashed walls and herringbone parquet flooring, and a long communal table runs through the centre, placing the emphasis on informal, shared dining. Expect dishes such as bruschetta with tofu, prawn and potato purée, and tuna *cotoletta* with ginger sauce. Wash it all down with a pokey *shochu* or single-malt whiskey from Yamazaki.
10 Via Vigevano, 20144
+ 39 02 836 0742
tokyotable.it

⑧
Trattoria Masuelli San Marco, Calvairate
Old and new

The signature dish may be *pasta e fagioli con il cucchiaio in piedi* – a pasta-and-bean affair so thick that a spoon will stand up in it – but Massimiliano Masuelli, chef and heir of this family enterprise that has been in business since 1921, generally aims for a lighter version of Milanese-Piedmontese fare. "Tradition is important but so is good digestion," he says.

If keeping things light is not your concern, settle down under the Gio Ponti-designed chandeliers and plump for the *risotto con ossobuco*.
80 Viale Umbria, 20135
+ 39 02 5518 4138
masuellitrattoria.com

⑨
Trippa, Porta Romana
Meat feast

With his handlebar moustache, gregarious nature and way with offal, Veneto native Diego Rossi (*pictured*) is one of the most popular chefs in town. "I wanted to open a proper trattoria," he says. "Our dishes are honest – what you see is what you get." You won't find a menu on the website as it changes depending on what's available at the market but the eponymous fried tripe, kidneys, liver, heart, lung and sweetbreads all feature heavily (less daring diners and vegetarians need not despair, there's also more standard fare available).

Overseeing front-of-house is Rossi's business partner Pietro Caroli, who will guide you through the mustard-yellow dining room. Securing a table can be tricky but there's a handy WhatsApp booking facility. Best seat in the house? At the kitchen-facing counter.
3 Via Giorgio Vasari, 20135
+39 327 668 7908
trippamilano.it

That looks terribly heavy. Let me help you

(11)
Trattoria del Pescatore, Bocconi
Fresh out of water

Huge loaves of bread are placed on every table in this traditional seafood restaurant and diners are fully encouraged to *fare la scarpetta* (mop up any leftover sauce). The pasta is handmade in the Sardinian hometown of owner Giuliano Ardu, whose wife Agnese helms the kitchen with their son. The latter interned at the three-Michelin-starred Arzak in San Sebastián and pushes the menu in a more contemporary direction.

The decor may leave a little to be desired but order the Catalan-style lobster with a bottle of something chilled from the impressive wine list and you won't even notice. It's almost impossible to find a table at the weekend so book well in advance.
5 Via Atto Vannucci, 20135
+39 02 5832 0452
trattoriadelpescatore.it

(10)
Spazio Milano, Duomo
Room with a view

Chef Niko Romito opened this attractive restaurant on the third floor of Autogrill's Mercato del Duomo in 2015. It's run by graduates of his culinary school in Abruzzo (next to his three-Michelin-starred restaurant) and boasts knockout views of the Galleria and Duomo.

Drag your gaze away from the floor-to-ceiling windows and you'll find dishes – from pappardelle with rabbit ragu, orange zest and pecorino cheese to ricotta-filled handmade tortelli with tomato juice and capers – that represent what Romito calls "the missing link between haute cuisine and simple home cooking". The Sala dell'Albero is the most spectacular space but if you're after a quieter experience ask to be seated in the second room.
3rd floor, Mercato del Duomo,
Galleria Vittorio Emanuele II, 20121
+39 02 878 400
nikoromito.com; ilmercatodelduomo.it

Day at the market
———
Chef Giuseppe Zen has three spots in the Mercato Comunale on the Darsena: Macelleria Popolare (meat), Resistenza Casearia (cheese) and Panificio Italiano (bread). Don't miss his *mondeghili* (Milanese meatballs) and lamb burger.
mangiaridistrada.com

Lunch
Take a break

Cashing in
—
The now leafy space used to house a bank

①

Soulgreen, Porta Nuova
Do it yourself

It would be easy to dismiss this vegan, gluten-free restaurant on the basis of its over-stylised interiors (think hanging succulents, artfully stripped walls and vast windows) but throw in attentive service and a tablet-based DIY ordering system and you have a smart lunch option in the shadow of Porta Nuova's gleaming skyscrapers.

Despite the health-conscious concept, dishes are both tasty and tasteful, with vivid salads, power bowls, soups and burgers influenced by the flavours of Asia, Mexico, the Mediterranean and the Middle East. There's also an extensive list of cold-pressed juices and smoothies. If all that sounds too wholesome, divert your attention to the selection of biodynamic wines from Italy, France and Australia.
Piazzale Principessa Clotilde, 20124
+39 02 6269 5162
soulgreen.com

Must-try
Risotto alla Milanese con ossobuco from Ratanà, Isola
Risotto is a staple of northern Italy. The Milanese version is imbued with saffron and generally served with *ossobuco* (veal shank). Chef Cesare Battisti at Ratanà has finessed the dish: "The secret is to use Lodigiano cheese, which is sweeter than Parmesan."
ratana.it

③ Latteria di San Marco, Porta Nuova
Dynamic duo

This tiny gem doesn't take reservations so you'll have to join the queue of regulars for your spot. And there's always a queue, such is the magic worked by Arturo and Maria Maggi (*pictured*): she oversees the tightly packed tables with her no-nonsense smile and signature pearl necklace while he, the "alchemist-cook", hides in the kitchen whipping up Italian classics with subtle twists.

The menu changes daily but there are a few staples such as the spaghetti with lemon and green chilli and a sumptuous crème caramel.
24 Via San Marco, 20121
+ 39 02 659 7653

② Un Posto a Milano, Porta Romana
Farm to table

The brainchild of the Esterni collective, this 18th-century farmhouse was restored in 2002 and today hosts a restaurant, bar, guesthouse, flower shop, bike shop and farmers' market.

Chef Nicola Cavallaro changes his menu according to what's in season: all produce is supplied by local farms. For lunch there's a buffet – with focaccia, *frittate*, pasta and vegetables – while dinner is à la carte. Young creatives and families flock to the generous, light-flooded communal spaces and double courtyard with vegetable patches.
2 Via Cuccagna, 20135
+ 39 02 545 7785
unpostoamilano.it

into the mix
Taglio is a restaurant, bar and shop in one

Fine dining

Milan became the birthplace of Italian contemporary fine dining when chef Gualtiero Marchesi returned from France in the 1970s, introducing elements of nouvelle cuisine into traditional Italian dishes. Today, the city boasts a swathe of smart options.

01 Il Luogo di Aimo e Nadia, Primaticcio
This restaurant has used great regional ingredients since 1962. Today Aimo Moroni's legacy is continued by chefs Negrini and Pisani.
aimoenadia.com

02 Ristorante Cracco, Cordusio
Milanese classics with a twist from Carlo Cracco. A new restaurant under the Galleria is opening soon.
ristorantecracco.it

03 D'O, San Pietro all'Olmo
Well worth the journey out of town.
cucinapop.do

04 Lume, San Cristoforo
Chef Luigi Taglienti's smart restaurant is set in a former factory.
lumemilano.com

05 Enrico Bartolini, Tortona
Innovative dishes and an elegant setting within the Mudec museum.
enricobartolini.net

Ⓢ
Temakinho, Porta Garibaldi
Natural instinct

This chain specialising in Japanese-Brazilian fusion has three locations (Porta Garibaldi, Magenta and Navigli) but the Corso Garibaldi venue near Brera tops our list. The tropical-themed decor forms the perfect backdrop to the made-to-order rolls, ceviches and tartares.

The house specialty is the *temaki*, a crunchy cone-shaped roll with a generous filling of rice, fresh branzino, tuna, salmon and various toppings. The caipirinha packs a punch so if a boozy lunch isn't on the cards stick to the detox-friendly tropical smoothies.
59 Corso Garibaldi, 20121
+ 39 02 7201 6158
temakinho.com

④
Taglio, Porta Genova
Roll on

Do as the locals do and order the *michetta* (Milan's typical flower-shaped bread roll) stuffed with mortadella. This will win you the favour of co-owner Raffaele Sangiovanni. There is also an impressive and ever-changing selection of cheese and cold cuts thanks to the partners' extensive and fiercely guarded contacts books.

For brunch choose the eggs Benedict washed down with something from the coffee menu, which beyond the ubiquitous espresso also includes AeroPress and Chemex.
10 Via Vigevano, 20144
+ 39 02 3653 4294
taglio.me

⑥
La Brisa, Cinque Vie
Quiet contender

This elegant restaurant, a long-time neighbourhood favourite, sits a stone's throw from Milan's Stock Exchange. The regulars – a mix of businessmen, ladies who lunch and families – favour it for the intimate garden and veranda, as well as chef Antonio Facciolo's seasonal and (mostly) light dishes. Wholewheat tagliatelle, broths and fish abound, though Facciolo also has a taste for guinea-fowl and crispy Iberian suckling pig. He slices the *culatello di Zibello* with a monumental Berkel that stands guard by the corner.
15 Via Brisa, 20123
+ 39 02 8645 0521
ristorantelabrisa.it

Peck

Since 1883, historic deli Peck has been the epitome of luxury gastronomy but with food-hall proportions: it occupies an entire building by the Duomo on Via Spadari. Meat is processed, charcuterie aged and fresh cheese made in the cellar; in the vast kitchens, shiny copper pots hang on immaculate walls; and the wine section features at least 3,000 labels. Each week it churns out 80kg of ragu and 100kg of braised beef for ravioli and pâté; each year it produces a staggering three tonnes of pesto, and confectionery is regularly shipped overseas.

Visit Peck on any given week and you'll find a happy mix of tourists, businessmen, retirees and artists. Grab a wedge of vacuum-packed Parmigiano Reggiano to take home and stop for a bite at the bistro. The only time to avoid it: Christmas Eve, when all of Milan arrives en masse to buy tortellini, chicken galantine, foie gras, cheese and cured meats.
peck.it

⑦
Pastamadre, Porta Romana
Eat like a Sicilian

Chef Francesco Costanzo's cooking focuses on his native Sicily's most iconic flavours, from tuna and octopus to pork and wild fennel. But don't go expecting a run-of-the-mill "regional" restaurant.

Sicily serves more as underlying inspiration – an excuse to dish up tangled heaps of freshly made pasta, plenty of fish and desserts such as *cassatina* (a creamy ricotta cake wrapped in green marzipan). These are dishes with a story and Costanzo will happily play the raconteur. Ask to hear the one about the cannoli moulds on the ceiling.
8 Via Bernardino Corio, 20135
+ 39 02 5519 0020

Regional produce
—
Milan has an endless supply of produce from its surrounding regions: gorgonzola, *bresaola* (dried, salted beef), Grana Padano, *mostarda di Cremona* (candied fruit and a mustard syrup), and Franciacorta sparkling wine are all worth sampling when in town.

Coffee shops
Beans around town

Bar Luce, Ripamonti
Picture perfect

Designed by Wes Anderson for Fondazione Prada (*see pages 94 and 103*), Bar Luce is classic Italian bar meets *The Grand Budapest Hotel*.

The interiors – with their vintage pinball machines, jukebox and bubblegum-pink, surgical-blue and acid-green palette – are pure 1950s kitsch. The details, from the Formica tables to the signature pastries made by Pasticceria Marchesi (*see page 40*), are as considered as props on a film set; the scene-stealing old Faema coffee machine operated by mustachioed waiters in bow ties is a favourite.
2 Largo Isarco, 20139
+39 02 5666 2611
fondazioneprada.org/barluce

Smell the roses
Grab a table among the fragrant flowers

Fioraio Bianchi Caffè, Porta Nuova
Best of the bunch

As the name suggests, this is first and foremost a flower shop but owner Raimondo Bianchi was inspired by the classic Parisian bistro. He opened the cosy venue on an elegant corner between San Fermo and Montebello in the 1970s and the *Milanesi bene* (the city's "old money") have long since adopted it as one of their own.

The café serves uncomplicated dishes for lunch and dinner but we prefer the mood in the morning: order a cappuccino then kick back and enjoy the unparalleled people-watching.
7 Via Montebello, 20121
+39 02 2901 4390
fioraiobianchicaffe.it

③
Upcycle, Città Studi
Wheel deal

In true Milanese fashion, this bike-themed café in Città Studi (the university district) is tucked away down an unassuming street behind a modest façade. The smart garage conversion doubles as a co-working space and serves breakfast, lunch and dinner to college students, freelancers and fans of the Giro d'Italia at long, communal tables.

Tools are available for impromptu fixes and there are maintenance courses as well as regular photography exhibitions and live music. Upcyle even produces its own line of cycling socks.
59 Via Andrea Maria Ampère, 20131
+ 39 02 8342 8268
upcyclecafe.it

> **Design files**
> Orsonero is all white walls and wooden counters

④
Orsonero Coffee, Porta Venezia
New direction

Canadian Brent Jopson opened Orsonero with his Milanese wife, pastry chef Giulia Gasperini, after identifying a gap in the market for speciality coffee. "We still sell more espressos than anything else but our customers are really starting to cotton on to the flat white," says Jopson. "The filtered coffee is also proving popular though sometimes I have to explain that it's not the same as an Americano."

The narrow, pared-back space overlooks a pleasant tree-lined street in the Porta Venezia area. Visit in the afternoon when the Milanese tend to be in less of a hurry.
15 Via Giuseppe Broggi, 20129
+ 39 366 547 7441

⑤

Pavè, Centrale
Paving the way

Friends Giovanni Giberti, Diego
Bamberghi and Luca Scanni
(*pictured, left to right*) have
turned Pavé into something of a
phenomenon. The on-site kitchen
is something that their *nonne* would
be proud of: a whirlwind of activity
churning out a neverending supply
of cakes, cookies, bread (they make
their own, naturally leavened) and
jam. They also serve some of the
city's most praised pastries, from
mille-feuille to panettone cooked
in glass jars.

The original Centrale venue
is popular with the area's young
professionals and a crowd of
regular pensioners, who cosy up
here to play the card game *briscola*.
Recently the trio have opened two
more locations, one in Porta Vittoria
serving gelato and the other, Pavè-
Break in Guastalla, focusing on
breakfast and take-away options.
27 Via Felice Casati, 20124
+39 02 9439 2259
pavemilano.com

Gelato

01 **Gelateria Umberto,
Guastalla:** This 1950s
ice-cream shop may only
offer a handful of flavours
but who cares when
they're this good? Try the
variations on *crema*: white,
yellow or with caramel.
+39 02 545 8113

02 **Antica Gelateria Sartori,
Centrale:** One of Milan's
best-kept secrets, this
1937 kiosk around the
corner from Stazione
Centrale is where the
locals gather on hot
summer nights. Try a
refreshing granita or
the Sicilian brioche filled
with classic flavours.
gelateriasartori.it

03 **Il Gelato Giusto, Porta
Venezia:** Vittoria
Bortolazzo has a chef's
approach to gelato:
exceptional ingredients,
creativity and elegance. If
available on the seasonally
changing menu, opt for
the basil, walnut and
chocolate sorbet.
gelatogiusto.it

04 **La Gelateria della
Musica, San Cristoforo:**
Located next to a red-
brick church on the *navigli*,
this spot is heaving during
the summer months. There
are lots of unique flavours
(bread, butter and jam,
anyone?) but our pick is
the salted pistachio.
lagelateriadellamusica.it

05 **Il Gelato Ecologico &
Frozen Yogurt, Wagner:**
This gelateria in a
residential neighbourhood
near Piazza Wagner
has long been using
all-natural ingredients.
Gluten-free, lactose-free
and certified kosher:
there's something for
everyone. We recommend
trying one of the chocolate
or soy flavours.
+39 02 4801 0917

Sweet treats
Caffè classici and pasticcerie

①

Pasticceria Marchesi, Cinque Vie
Perfect pastries

Of all the *pasticcerie* in town, this is the most iconic: the 18th-century palazzo, with its coffered ceiling and façade emblazoned with gold script, is worth a visit alone. Inside, naturally leavened brioches compete with *veneziane* (cream-filled fritters) and jars of dragees.

In 2014, Marchesi was acquired by the Prada Group, resulting in two more locations – one on Via Montenapoleone and the other inside the Galleria Vittorio Emanuele II – but this is by far the best.

*11A Via Santa Maria alla Porta,
20123*
+39 02 862 770
pasticceriamarchesi.com

②

Cova, Quadrilatero della Moda
Old favourite

Over the course of its 200-year history, Cova has seen the likes of Giuseppe Verdi and Giacomo Puccini saunter through its doors. Originally located on the corner of Piazza della Scala, the *pasticceria* relocated to its current address on Milan's chicest street in the 1950s.

The majority owner is now LVMH and a sensitive renovation has ensured that the spirit remains intact, the service impeccable and the pastries of the highest quality. The interior is equally flawless: note the marble-and-mahogany centrepiece counter.

8 Via Montenapoleone, 20121
+39 02 7600 5599
covamilano.com

③

Taveggia Milano 1909, Monforte
Coffee and croissants

Taveggia first threw open its doors in 1909: the year of Marinetti's *Manifesto del Futurismo*, as power lines and factories were springing up across the city and change was afoot.

For more than a century the café has continued to lure visitors with its legendary rice pudding and 30 different types of brioche. The coffee is a special house blend best savoured in the tearoom, which looks exactly as it did in 1954. Gather under the crystal chandeliers and order an Americano with a savoury pastry.

*2 Via Uberto Visconti di Modrone,
20122*
+39 02 7628 0856
taveggia.it

⑤
Gattullo, Bocconi
Cake or cocktail?

The Gattullo family has been baking fine cakes and pastries at this old-school *pasticceria* near the Università Bocconi (*see page 105*) since 1961 and is perennially popular with professors, students and jazz musicians.

Order the *crostata di crema* (custard tart) or, if 'tis the season, the famed panettone, prepared on the premises over the course of two days using candied Italian citrus fruits and Turkish sultanas. If pastries aren't your bag, make a beeline for the walnut-panelled bar and sink a Campari spritz.

2 Piazzale di Porta Lodovica, 20136
+39 02 5831 0497
gattullo.it

Must-try
Panettone from
Pasticceria Martesana
Milano, Maggiolina
Traditionally a Christmas treat, this fluffy masterpiece of eggs, butter, candied fruit and raisins can now be found almost all year round. Grab yours from award-winning Martesana Milano, founded in 1966 near one of Milan's *navigli*.
martesanamilano.com

④

Pasticceria Sissi, Risorgimento
Best for brioches

The name Sissi is more than just a tribute to the legendary Austrian empress whose portrait adorns the sign above the door: it's that of the lady who opened this pint-sized *pasticceria* in the early 1990s with her Senegalese husband.

You'll find all the classics – from cream puffs to fruit tarts – though the real treat is sitting in the back, under the pergola, and eating one of the house brioches, which are freshly made on-site each day: the sweet ones are filled to order with custard or chocolate cream, while the savoury ones are stuffed with prosciutto.

6 Piazza Risorgimento, 20129
+39 02 7601 4664

⑥
Cucchi, Porta Genova
Part of the charm

On weekend mornings, writers and journalists rub shoulders with designers in Supreme T-shirts and lawyers in Zegna suits at Cucchi's outdoor seating area. Grab a table kerbside with this eclectic crowd and you might hear the bells of Sant'Ambrogio strike the hour.

Sure, the tartines may look as though they've jumped out of a 1970s spread of *La Cucina Italiana*, and the decor hovers somewhere between granny-chic and kitsch, but Cucchi has been operating since 1936 so a few things can be forgiven.

1 Corso Genova, 20123
+39 02 8940 9793
pasticceriacucchi.it

Aperitivo
Campari o'clock

01

02 03

04 05

06

07 08

09

n'ombra de vin enoteca

10

11   12

Order of the day

Milan boasts a vibrant aperitivo scene but there are some unspoken rules to follow when it comes to those all-important pre-dinner drinks and nibbles. The first is timing: you're unlikely to find anyone reaching for the glass before 18.00. Tradition warrants Campari, Aperol or vermouth-based cocktails such as a negroni or spritz and, remember, any more than two or three rounds might raise eyebrows. Most bars in the city will offer some form of aperitivo but here are a few of our favourite haunts.

01 — 03 Bottiglieria Bulloni, La Maddalena
Blue and white-collar workers sit cheek-to-cheek at the small tables of this classic 1930s *bottiglieria* (bottle shop) with barrels of soul.
+39 02 4800 3155

04 — 05 Cantine Isola, Sarpi
There's a homely atmosphere at this wine bar in the heart of Chinatown, which is much loved by connoisseurs.
+39 02 331 5249

06 — 08 El Büscia, Bocconi
This wine shop near the Università Bocconi (*see page 105*) specialises in sparkling wines. Drop by and grab yourself a bottle of bubbly.
elbuscia.it

09 — 10 N'Ombra de Vin, Porta Nuova
Below the streets of Porta Nuova this spacious yet cosy vaulted cellar is where the hip kids of Milan meet and mingle.
nombradevin.it

11 — 12 Bicerin, Porta Venezia
Industrial meets vintage at this well-stocked wineroom (the shelves boast more than 800 labels) in the diverse Porta Venezia area.
bicerinmilano.com

Drinks
Raise a glass

Frida, Isola
Cool courtyard

Frida was hip long before the Isola neighbourhood (*see page 130*), which is separated from the rest of the city by the train tracks of Porta Garibaldi, caught up with it. Today the spacious courtyard, dripping with vines, attracts a mixed crowd of artists, students and creatives.

There are more than 80 cocktails on the menu and a strong selection of artisanal beers. Of course, you can always order a *birretta* (small beer) or, if you're feeling brave, opt for one of the absinthe-based drinks.
*3 Via Antonio Pollaiuolo, 20159
+39 02 680 260
fridaisola.it*

2
Rita & Cocktails, Navigli
Raising the bar

Prompted by the lack of decent cocktail bars in the city, Edoardo Nono opened this joint – known simply as Rita – with business partner and chef Gianluca Chiaruttini in 2002. "Fifteen years ago Italian cocktail bars were more concerned with quantity than quality," says Nono. "We wanted to open our own, which focused on great quality, fresh ingredients."

There's no showmanship here, just smart service and clever flavour combinations. Don't sit at a table: pull up a stool at the bespoke wooden bar and tell the staff what tickles your fancy.
*1 Via Angelo Fumagalli, 20143
+39 02 837 2865*

③
Otto, Sarpi
Day and night

Set on a small square off Via Paolo Sarpi in the heart of lively Chinatown, this light-drenched space packed with tropical plants and mismatched vintage furniture is a favourite among the city's freelancers, who flock here for the *taglieri* (platters) and ubiquitous avocado-and-feta toast.

Come evening, once the laptops have been safely stashed away, the drinks flow freely and the tapping of keyboards is replaced with cheery chatter. In the summer months snatch one of the sought-after seats on the outdoor deck and order the house gin and tonic.
8 Via Paolo Sarpi, 20154
sarpiotto.com

④

The Botanical Club, Isola
It takes two

Unstoppable duo Alessandro Longhin and Davide Martelli opened The Botanical Club, which hosts Italy's first gin micro-distillery, in Isola in 2015. A second, larger location equipped with a poke bar followed in Tortona and they have since launched martini bar Idéal and natural wine bar Champagne Socialist at other locations across the city.

Head to the original venue for their new wave negroni made with mezcal, hints of black pepper and garlic.
11 Via Pastrengo, 20159
+ 39 02 3652 3846
thebotanicalclub.com

⑤

Ceresio 7, Sarpi
Fashion fix

With its two pools, wrap-around terrace with striking views, cigar room and sleek interiors courtesy of DimoreStudio (*see page 52*), it's not hard to see why the crowds flock to this lofty venue owned by Canadian fashion designers Dean and Dan Caten (the Milan headquarters for their label Dsquared2 is next door).

Try the Resio C'è, created by bartender Guglielmo Miriello, with the vegetable chips or fresh focaccia with mortadella. There's also a gym and spa on-site (*see page 124*).
7 Via Ceresio, 20154
+ 39 02 3103 9221
ceresio7.com

6 Bar Basso, Città Studi
Celebrated crowd

During the Salone del Mobile this is the after-party venue of choice, with an electric atmosphere and lengthy queues. Hemingway was once a regular, as were many famous actors, gangsters and even Italian presidents, fraternising with the students of the nearby Politecnico di Milano at the first non-hotel cocktail bar in the city.

Order the negroni sbagliato ("wrong" negroni), which was born when legendary barman Mirko Stocchetto – who cut his teeth at Harry's Bar in Venice – accidentally mixed *spumante* instead of gin with the Campari and vermouth. To this day it's served in bucket-sized glasses by Stocchetto's son Maurizio (*pictured*). Don't miss the collection of old wine glasses, cups, highballs and flutes. And no need to give your taxi driver the address: everybody knows where it is.
39 Via Plinio, 20020
+ 39 02 2940 0580
barbasso.com

We like to party, look!

Retail
—— Shop assistance

A common attitude among visitors to Milan is that they've come here to shop and nothing else (honestly, what about visiting the Pinacoteca di Brera or the Triennale di Milano?) but let's not get too indignant: it's only right that the city's world-famous retail offerings should be indulged, and these pages will see that you make the most of them.

Milan is home to prestigious names such as Prada and Caruso and, while we've raised our hats to these old friends (speaking of hats, don't miss Borsalino), we've also sought out the lone craftsmen, the tucked-away tailors and the independent bookshops in which to while away a rainy afternoon.

So fear not if the city seems awash with shops and shoppers: we'll guide you across the ocean of big-name brands and steer you towards the best of them.

①
Spazio Rossana Orlandi,
Sant'Ambrogio
Design hub

Rossana Orlandi (*pictured*) has established herself as the guru of the Milanese scene, launching emerging designers with her renowned and offbeat taste for new ideas.

A warren of ever-changing installations by talents such as Piet Hein Eek, Nacho Carbonell and Maarten Baas surrounds Orlandi's covered courtyard, which acts as a living room for Milan's design world. "It's more than a gallery," says Orlandi. "It's a design hub – a space to experience design with an open mind."
14-16 Via Matteo Bandello, 20123
+ 39 02 467 4471
rossanaorlandi.com

②

Nilufar Depot, Derganino
Open house

Since opening in 2015, this sprawling, three-storey space has dazzled aesthetes. "A vintage touch keeps a modern room from being too monotonous," says gallerist and owner Nina Yashar, who combines 20th-century Italian furniture with cutting-edge pieces from contemporary designers.

Her choices – from the likes of Cristina Celestino and Lindsey Adelman – are as visually appealing as they are practical and the space was designed by Massimiliano Locatelli to mirror the decadence of La Scala.
34 Viale Vincenzo Lancetti, 20158
+ 39 02 3659 0800
nilufar.com

Under the influence

When Carla Sozzani opened 10 Corso Como in 1990, it was the world's first concept store. Adventurous choices made it a destination for the international fashion set and it has now been acquired by two entrepreneurs set to continue its influential trajectory.
10corsocomo.com

③
Artemide, Monforte
Lightbulb moments

Founded in 1960 by Ernesto
Gismondi, lighting manufacturer
Artemide has worked with such
eminent talents as Ettore Sottsass,
Daniel Libeskind, Santiago
Calatrava and Mario Botta.

Here you'll find pieces of
design history including Michele
De Lucchi's Tolomeo light (in
all of its forms and guises), Vico
Magistretti's Eclisse table lamp
and Richard Sapper's angled
Tizio. The showroom's ceiling is
just the right height to enjoy the
striking collection of pendant
lights. Illuminating stuff.
19 Corso Monforte, 20122
+ 39 02 7600 6930
artemide.com

④
Eligo, Porta Garibaldi
Revitalising tradition

Eligo brings together distinctive
objects and crafts from regions
across the Italian peninsula –
the pewter of Brescia, the green
glass of Empoli and the baskets
of Sardinia – alongside classic
pieces reworked with an eye for
contemporary aesthetics.

It's all in an effort to breathe
new life into Italy's design heritage:
for instance, in the hands of Eligo's
three designers, the Tigullina
armchair from the Chiavari
collection has been brought back
into production after 50 years.
View the designs by appointment.
8 Via Palermo, 20121
+ 39 02 8396 2003
eligo.it

⑤
Cassina, San Babila
Prestigious products

Cassina, a staple of the Lombard
design scene, was founded in Meda
on the outskirts of the city in 1927.
This showroom, on the furniture
district's main drag, opened in
1968 and was designed by Milanese
architect-designer Mario Bellini.
It has since been overhauled by
a posse of design heavyweights
including Vico Magistretti,
Clino Trini Castelli and Achille
Castiglioni. Today, art director
Patricia Urquiola has brought her
own distinctive brand of bold,
colourful warmth to the space.

In recent years Cassina has
commissioned some of the
industry's biggest names, including
Konstantin Grcic, the Bouroullec
Brothers, Jaime Hayon and, of
course, Urquiola herself. It also
continues to reproduce classic
pieces such as Le Corbusier's
LC4 chaise longue.
16 Via Durini, 20122
+ 39 02 7602 0745
cassina.com

Blast of colour
———

Ettore Sottsass (*see page
110*) founded the flamboyant
Memphis movement in the
early 1980s and you can find
his idiosyncratic designs –
alongside those by others such
as Marco Zanini – at the Post
Design Gallery (the Memphis
showroom) in Porta Nuova.
memphis-milano.com

⑥ Spotti, Porta Venezia
Stand-out spaces

This design gallery has remained a rigorously contemporary outpost since it opened in 1986. From accessories to furniture installations, Spotti is filled with pieces from the likes of Agape and Arper, plus reissues of iconic designs by Lina Bo Bardi and Gio Ponti.

Seasonal makeovers by local design firm Studiopepe transform the shop into a dynamic series of enviable living rooms that stand out for their distinctly Milanese style and captivating colour palettes.
27 Viale Piave, 20129
+39 02 781 953
spotti.com

⑦ Raimondo Garau, Porta Garibaldi
Hunter gatherer

An antiquities collector since the 1980s, Raimondo Garau (*pictured*) hunts around Italy and beyond for everything from 18th-century armoires to 1950s armchairs. Inside this glass-walled space the selection of lamps, carpets, tables and chairs is always surprising thanks to the owner's unexpected (and sometimes brave) pairings.

Garau's stockroom is a treasure trove of pieces which are either yet to surface for display or ready to be shipped to the international aficionados who come here from around the world.
5B Viale Francesco Crispi, 20121
+39 02 659 9913
raimondogarau.com

You know, I think we've found our perch!

Four design monobrands

There are entire swathes of Milan dedicated to design brands and their showrooms: a stroll around the area of Via Durini, Corso Europa and Corso Monforte will lead you to many of the biggest names. Here are four that are likely to inspire an impromptu home-interior overhaul.

01 Flos, Monforte: This whitewashed space on Corso Monforte was designed by Jasper Morrison. You'll find classics such as Achille Castiglioni's stringy Parentesi lamp and more recent lighting designs such as Extra T by Michael Anastassiades.
flos.com

02 Molteni&C, San Babila: This huge Vincent van Duysen-designed flagship on Corso Europa is shared with sister brand Dada. Don't miss re-issued Gio Ponti masterpieces such as the classy D.655.1 chest of drawers.
molteni.it

03 DePadova, Monforte: Designed by Piero Lissoni, this loft on Via Santa Cecilia hosts bathrooms and kitchens by Boffi (with which DePadova recently merged). Try the cosy Yak sofa by LucidiPevere.
depadova.com

04 B&B Italia, San Babila: At its Renzo Piano and Richard Rogers-designed HQ near Como, B&B Italia creates a multitude of timeless furniture and homeware, often in collaboration with big names such as Antonio Citterio and David Chipperfield. You'll find all of these and more at its showroom on Via Durini.
bebitalia.com

8

DimoreGallery, Brera
Maximum charm

American Britt Moran and Italian Emiliano Salci are the brains behind DimoreStudio, best known for its bold, experimental furniture and bespoke interiors with a heavy dose of 1970s chic.

This, their whimsical showroom in a capacious apartment on Via Solferino features the duo's own collections, as well as vintage pieces such as Gio Ponti armchairs, which they have reimagined. The unashamedly maximalist arrangements will charm even the most staunch minimalist. All items in the studio are for sale.
11 Via Solferino, 20121
+ 39 02 3656 3420
dimoregallery.com

Specialist retail
Dedicated ranges

①

Fratelli Bonvini, Ripamonti
The write stuff

The 117 pea-green drawers behind the dark wooden counter at Fratelli Bonvini are home to all manner of stationery items from across the past century (25 of them alone are dedicated to pen nibs).

First opened in 1909, the shop was rescued from closure in 2012 by five publishing buffs who maintained its vintage signage and hefty letterpress. From almond-scented Coccoina glue and brass pencil sharpeners to 1950s notepaper and the ubiquitous Staedtler eraser, any writer's needs (fancy or mundane) are covered.
1 Via Tagliamento, 20139
+ 39 02 539 2151
bonvini1909.com

③ Preattoni, Quadrilatero della Moda
Cutting-edge

An old-school knife and grooming specialist (*coltelleria*), this shop owned by Lorenzo Preattoni (*pictured*) is lined with gleaming razors, hard-to-find perfumes and honed kitchen knives.

The *coltelleria* is a Milanese institution and this one has been at its apex since it was founded by Pietro Preattoni in 1902. Clients trek from neighbouring cities for its Mühle shaving kits, beaver brushes from London-based Simpsons, Solingen knives and scents by Creed and Panama from Paris and Naples.

52 Via della Spiga, 20121
+39 02 7600 1059
preattoni.it

②
Foto Veneta Ottica, Carrobio
A visual focus

Born in 1931 as a photo studio (mainly taking passport shots), this is now one of Europe's leading purveyors of vintage eyewear. That's not to say that the pieces are second-hand: founder Gabriele Bisello's son Giorgio (*pictured*) and grandson Emanuele source new but leftover stock from around the world to sit beside modern labels such as Germano Gambini.

Their eyewear has appeared in films and on magazine covers from *Vogue* to *Vanity Fair* but the Bisellos haven't forgotten their roots: they'll still take your passport snap.

57 Via Torino, 20123
+39 02 805 5735
fotovenetaottica.com

Look sharp

When Milan's legendary knifemaker Aldo Lorenzi fell on hard times, Guglielmo Miani of menswear brand Larusmiani helped save the century-old artisan. You'll find the new workshop and full collection at Larusmiani's Montenapoleone flagship.
larusmiani.it

④

Potafiori, Bocconi
Flowers, food and feel-good sounds

This flower shop and café was opened in 2015 by Rosalba Piccinni (*pictured*). The flowers and bouquets that serve as luscious decoration are all for sale, while concrete walls, expansive windows and William Morris prints complete the interior.

There's a bistro that's open for coffee, lunch and dinner with a menu that changes weekly depending on seasonal availability. Thursday evenings mean live jazz sessions – Piccinni is a singer herself, so you may even catch her at the mic.
17 Via Salasco, 20136
+ 39 02 8706 5930
potafiori.com

⑤

Borsalino, Quadrilatero della Moda
Head start

Giuseppe Borsalino set the standard for modern hat-making when he opened his atelier in Alessandria, Piedmont, in 1857. Since then, icons from Marcello Mastroianni to Robert Redford have sported the shop's headwear.

The flagship carries pieces for men and women, and allows customers to select everything from brim width to silk lining. Look out for the frequent collaborations such as the colourful, plumed collection by Californian hatmaker Nick Fouquet.
5 Via Sant'Andrea, 20121
+ 39 02 7601 7072
borsalino.com

⑥
Fontana Milano 1915,
Porta Romana
In the bag

As its name suggests, Fontana
was founded in 1915 by Guido
Pieracci – albeit in Florence. After
the Second World War the company
moved to Milan under Pieracci's
son-in-law, Carlo Massa, who set
up the current HQ on Via Trebbia.

The ivy-framed shop is
accessed via an inner courtyard;
the renowned leather purses,
messenger bags and accessories
are today made by Massa's sons,
Michele and Paolo, in the upstairs
atelier (it occupies almost the
length of the street).
26 Via Trebbia, 20135
+39 02 5403 02359
fontanamilano1915.com

①
Micamera, Isola
Picture this

This bookshop contains some
5,000 titles on photography
focusing on US shutterbugs from
the 1970s onwards. One of Italy's
finest specialists in the genre, it
attracted cool cats long before
Isola itself became a trendsetter.

Owners Flavio Franzoni and
Giulia Zorzi regularly organise
exhibitions and workshops
with photographers and editors.
Franzoni also helps young snappers
get their work in to print; find them
alongside treasures by William
Eggleston and Antoine d'Agata.
19 Via Medardo Rosso, 20159
+39 02 4548 1569
micamera.it

②

Gogol & Company, Giambellino
Coffee culture

This literary coffee shop was born
in 2010 when a group of friends
decided to share their passion for
books. Spread across two floors,
the selection covers everything
from graphic novels and classics
to new titles by independent
publishing houses such as Milan-
based Nottetempo.

A smattering of armchairs and
tables means that you can devour a
novel while savouring a double-
butter croissant; everything on
the daily menu is made in-house.
Evening events range from literary
debates to jazz-and-wine soirées.
101 Via Savona, 20144
+ 39 02 4547 0449
gogolandcompany.com

③

121+, Tortona
Pop-up turned permanent

Originally a temporary project
intended to stay open for 121 days,
this bookshop became a permanent
affair – hence its name. A retail
outlet of publishing house Corraini,
it sells much of its own catalogue,
including a hefty number of titles
by Milanese designer Bruno
Munari, famed for his children's
books and flair with graphic design.

Illustrated books are an obvious
focus but there are also design,
architecture, photography, fashion,
cooking and gardening volumes,
while the walls feature a changing
selection of artworks.
17 Via Savona, 20144
+ 39 02 3658 4119
corraini.com

Menswear
Suits you

❸
Sunnei, Città Studi
Youthful and modern

This tiny space allows you to browse the Sunnei collections with founders Simone Rizzo and Loris Messina (*pictured, Rizzo on right*) on hand. "You can find us here, along with pieces from our line not available elsewhere," says Rizzo.

The brand's modern look (think colourful shirts and trousers) is echoed in the Studio Modulo-designed space; the youthful vision of the designers is evident in the select range of magazines and their occasional beer-fuelled fêtes.
8 Via Vincenzo Vela, 20133
+39 02 2951 1728
sunnei.it

❹
Full, Porta Venezia
Smart selection

In a city dominated by monobrand boutiques, shop owner Luca Santamaria is to be congratulated on his tasteful selection of menswear. Full carries a range of hard-to-find labels selected for their quality and good fit.

Pick out smart-looking shirts from ABCL (a Venetian brand that fuses Italian design with Japanese fabrics such as selvedge cotton), belts from Milanese designer Adriano Meneghetti and jackets by Massimo Piombo. Santamaria has also now introduced a tailoring service for customers in need of a bespoke suit or jacket.
11 Via Lambro, 20129
+39 02 2951 1229

②
A Caraceni, Brera
Bespoke only

The Caraceni brothers were perhaps Italy's best tailors and A Caraceni was opened by Augusto, who returned to Milan from Paris at the beginning of the Second World War. Today it's run by Carlo Andreacchio and son Massimiliano (*both pictured*) and is bespoke only, with clients such as Karl Lagerfeld, Ralph Lauren and Gianni Agnelli.

"Our suits are as comfortable as pyjamas," says Carlo. A two-piece requires some 60 hours of work and features a secret Caraceni weave handed down from maestro to maestro.
16 Via Fatebenefratelli, 20121
+39 02 655 1972
caracenimilano.com

❶
Caruso, Quadrilatero della Moda
Dramatic looks

Caruso's flagship store is almost as impressive as its clothes. The theme is "backstage at the theatre" (the brand name is partly inspired by Italian tenor Enrico Caruso), with ropes, pulleys, red-velvet curtains and an appropriately grand wardrobe for the client-protagonist.

The shop has three salons, with one dedicated to formal evening-wear. Both ready-to-wear and made-to-measure suits are available in fabrics ranging from Quattroventi (a crease-resistant, two-ply yarn) to the label's supersoft Gobigold camel wool.
4 Via Gesù, 20121
+39 02 7634 0496
carusomenswear.com

⑥
Sciamat, Quadrilatero della Moda
Shouldering responsibility

This small but formidable tailor was established by Valentino and Nicola Ricci; frustrated with hackneyed tailors who refused to accommodate their requests, the brothers ditched their jobs in law and finance to do it themselves.

Nicola mans the showroom while Valentino weaves away in their Puglia atelier. The self-taught maestro achieves a close and broad-shouldered fit (the "Sciamat" shoulder) with little structure and padding. "It looks rigid but feel how pliant it is," says Nicola, rolling a jacket into a ball.

19 Via Montenapoleone, 20121
+ 39 080 371 5426
sciamat.com

⑤
Slowear, Porta Nuova
Mixed ingredients

Fashion powerhouse Slowear owns a stable of speciality menswear brands, each of which focuses on a single product and avoids following fickle fashion trends.

At its Milan flagship, complete with plush carpets and exposed brick walls, shoppers will find smart chinos and trousers from its Incotex line, unstructured jackets for all seasons by Montedoro together with sophisticated knitwear from Zanone and a rich assortment of classy button-down shirts.

18 Via Solferino, 20121
+ 39 02 6347 1384
slowear.com

❶
Velasca, Sempione
Calfskin creations

Unable to find luxury shoes without a hefty price tag, friends Jacopo Sebastio and Enrico Casati (*pictured, Sebastio on left*) travelled to Italy's shoe-making capital, the Marche region, to establish their own label and style. Each pair is made from French calfskin in the town of Montegranaro. Their preferred construction is the Blake-Rapid: a slimmer silhouette to the Goodyear Welt.

Despite its Marche provenance, the brand set up shop near Milan's tranquil Parco Sempione and a Rome outpost followed shortly after.

2 Piazza Sempione, 20154
+ 39 338 945 7733
velasca.com

②
Rivolta, Quadrilatero della Moda
Sole traders

Rivolta has been hand-making bespoke shoes since 1883, when Enrico Rivolta sold his first pair. In recent years his descendant Fabrizio and wife Manuela introduced a ready-to-wear line for men and women. "The style is purely Milanese, sturdy and elegant," says Manuela.

Any whim or desire is catered for, including crocodile leather. And to ensure a perfect fit, a 3D scanner measures the patron's feet three times. The prêt-a-porter range features a lightweight line of suede loafers known as Aria.
17 Via della Spiga, 20121
+ 39 02 798 751
calzoleriarivolta.com

③
Stivaleria Savoia, Magenta
Old-school atelier

This shoemaker, which started off making boots for the Savoia Cavalleria regiment, is one of the last Milanese brands to fashion footwear without any machinery whatsoever – you can see the workspace and tools at the back of the atelier.

Bespoke shoes are made in all materials and styles and there's a ready-to-wear line too, as well as leather bags and belts. The shop also occasionally hosts Varese-based Sartoria Vergallo, should you need a bespoke suit to match the brogues.
8 Via Vincenzo Monti, 20123
+ 39 02 463 424
stivaleriasavoia.it

Mixed
Something for everyone

①
Aspesi, Quadrilatero della Moda
No go for logos

While luxury brands dominate the Via Montenapoleone shopfronts, Aspesi has carved out a niche here thanks to its refreshing approach to retail. Housed in a sprawling space, it sports a dressing room in a shipping container and is known for its quirky window displays.

The label's basics for men and women are a hit with locals, the big draw being its logo-free outerwear consisting of everything from windbreakers to heavier jackets in understated shades of blue and green, made with top-end technical fabrics.
13 Via Montenapoleone, 20121
+ 39 02 7602 2478
aspesi.com

2

Biffi, Porta Genova
Milan institution

Opened by sisters Rosy and Adele
Biffi, this shop has been a steady
presence on Milan's fashion scene
since the 1960s. Its brightly lit,
two-floor contemporary space was
designed by Toni Cordero.

On the shelves you'll find both
men's and womenswear brands
such as Thom Browne, Comme
des Garçons, Barena and even
Japanese designer Junya Watanabe.
Biffi also has three other locations:
B-Contemporary, the menswear
spot across the street from the
flagship, carries sportier brands
such as Golden Goose and Sun68.
6 Corso Genova, 20123
+ 39 02 8311 6052
biffi.com

3

Boglioli, Quadrilatero della Moda
Laidback and luxurious

Boglioli celebrates classic Milanese
style: elegant, structured and
never ostentatious. The menswear
brand offers a modern take on
nonchalant luxury, typical of the
1960s Milanese man-about-town.
Cashmere silk-blend jackets, classic
cotton chinos and close-fitting suits
assume a colour palette that echoes
the city's muted tones.

The space, designed by the
nearby DimoreStudio (*see page
52*), is as elegant as the collection:
a lounge-like environment of wood-
panelled walls, warm lights and
marble floors.
17 Via San Pietro all'Orto, 20121
+ 39 02 7639 4051
boglioli.it

A passion for fashion

Each of the world's four
fashion capitals has its thing:
Paris has haute couture;
London, experimental
youthfulness; New York,
trend-driven commercialism.
And Milan? Milan has big,
bold, family-run Italian labels.

The city leapt onto the
global style map in 1958 when
it staged its first fashion week.
And while it has a rich heritage
in manufacturing and tailoring,
it's Milan's luxury fashion
houses (and the larger-than-life
personalities behind them) that
fuel its sartorial scene: Giorgio
Armani has long been a pioneer
for Milan's fashion agenda, as
have the likes of Gildo Zegna
and the Prada family.

The city dons its best attire
four times a year: in January
and June for men's week, and
February and September for
women's. Shows are staged
in historic buildings such as the
renaissance-style Università
Statale and streets become
overrun with flashbulbs and
fans (Armani tends to draw the
most frenzied crowds).

Milan's fashion pedigree
has encouraged a number of
other Italian fashion houses
to flock to the city, building
palatial shops around Via
Montenapoleone. Here are
three more worth noting:

01 Gucci, Quadrilatero
della Moda: The
Florentine label excels
in leather goods.
gucci.com

02 Salvatore Ferragamo,
Quadrilatero della Moda:
Mid-century cool and
colour from Rome.
ferragamo.com

03 Tod's, Quadrilatero
della Moda: This
family-owned brand
sets the standard for
moccasins.
tods.com

④

Dictionary, Porta Genova
Word on the street

Don't assume that this is just
another of the skating shops that
abound near the Colonne di San
Lorenzo: behind the tiny shopfront
you'll find much more refined and
design-conscious clothing.

Dictionary's range straddles
streetwear and contemporary
fashion: the brand selection is
Scandi-heavy (or at least Scandi-
inspired) with the likes of Norse
Projects; Biella-based Camo is
the lone (but worthy) Italian
label. Accessories on offer include
Sandqvist bags and Suicoke
sandals from Japan.
46 Corso di Porta Ticinese, 20123
+39 02 835 8212
dictionarymilano.it

*Now this is
shopping
in style...*

⑤

Massimo Alba, Brera
Dream weaver

Known for his knack with cashmere,
Massimo Alba is right at home
weaving knitwear for men and
women – and winning plaudits
for his collections of superbly soft
garments. His Italian cashmere is
dyed with chemical-free pigments.

Fans flock to the Brera boutique,
where an old-fashioned shop bell
announces your arrival. Besides the
jumpers and cardigans you'll find
slim trousers, unstructured jackets
and casual shirts in luxurious
cotton and linens and an array
of subtle pastel tones.
8 Via Brera, 20121
+39 02 7209 3420
massimoalba.com

Layer up
———
In need of a new coat? Head
to either Valstar or Sealup.
The former, a recent men's
label, makes suede and leather
bomber jackets. The latter
has been around since 1935
and offers classic macs and
overcoats for both men
and women.
valstar.it; sealup.net

⑥
Nonostante Marras, Tortona
Vibrant vintage

A former factory, Nonostante Marras doesn't really feel like a shop, which is just how Antonio Marras likes it. The Sardinian designer has filled his fanciful emporium with vintage objects to create a richly cosy environment.

"I like to take things that seem to be in conflict with each other and create a dialogue between them," says Marras. His theatrical space features books, dim chandeliers and places to relax while contemplating the clothes.
8 Via Cola di Rienzo, 20144
+ 39 02 8907 5002
antoniomarras.it

⑦
Pupi Solari & Host, Magenta
Elegant options

Eighty-something fashion doyenne Pupi Solari opened her first boutique in 1969. Today, the Genoa native oversees an enviable trio of clothing shops (one each for men, women and children) overlooking one of Milan's prettiest piazzas.

At her eponymous space for women, Solari carries a trove of elegant pieces, with brands ranging from Dusan to silk experts Mantero. For youngsters there are pastel play-clothes that parents can't resist while at her menswear shop, Host, there's knitwear from Altea, casual shirts from Bevilacqua and jackets by Caruso.
2 Piazza Nicolò Tommaseo, 20123
+ 39 02 463 325
pupisolari.com

Prada, Duomo
Big-name brand

In 2013, Prada opened a second space in the Galleria Vittorio Emanuele II, opposite its historic location under the arcade's glass dome. The boutiques offer an insight into the world of Mario Prada: think Golden Malacca canes and shagreen walking-sticks, mahogany furniture, Belgian marble and painted panels by La Scala's principal scenographer Nicola Benois.
Menswear: 62 Galleria Vittorio
Emanuele II, 20121
+ 39 02 8721 1450
Womenswear: 63 Galleria Vittorio
Emanuele II, 20121
+ 39 02 876 979
prada.com

Womenswear
Fashionable choices

Wait and See, Cinque Vie
Convent conversion

On the ground floor of a former 18th-century convent, Wait and See is stuffed with colourfully jubilant vintage and contemporary fashion handpicked by owner Uberta Zambeletti (*pictured*).

Among the exotic treasures from far-flung bazaars and vibrant-toned frocks from niche labels, there is a wealth of pieces created specially for the shop. Images of the Virgin Mary and strings of pennant flags decorate the interior, while a giant wheel spins the jewellery selection like roulette. It may sound gaudy but this space has a winning charm.
14 Via Santa Marta, 20123
+39 02 7208 0195
waitandsee.it

No30, Quadrilatero della Moda
Top of the lines

Concealed in an inner courtyard, away from the big monobrand shops that line Via della Spiga, No30's unique stable of designers has been attracting loyalists since 2008.

An inspired selection of high-end womenswear reflects the heart and soul of this boutique. "Passion – for both the clients and the clothing – comes before our commercial concerns," says owner Ezia Degiovannini, who picks her range from top labels and future design stars (Antonio Berardi and Comeforbreakfast among them).
30 Via della Spiga, 20121
+39 02 7631 7377
n30milano.com

Lap of luxury
——
Italian fashion is synonymous with Giorgio Armani. Since launching his first collection in 1975, the eponymous brand has grown into one of the most prestigious names in fashion and expanded into hotels, homeware and even flowers.
armani.com

Tearose, Quadrilatero della Moda
Blooming marvellous

Founded by Alessandra Rovati Vitali more than 20 years ago, this two-storey emporium began as a contemporary florist but later added fashion, fragrances and homeware to its roster; Ulrika Lundgren's brand, Rika, is our pick.

The artisan perfume selection and seasonal blooms fill the shop with an ethereal scent that underscores the romantic mix of clothes – chic but garden-friendly frocks from Italian and international designers that are perfectly suited for a grand Italian wedding.
27 Manzoni, 20121
+39 02 8699 8767
tearose.it

Things we'd buy
—— Shop front

While Paris and London offer retail therapy, Milan provides a retail cure. Its superlative spread – tailored clothes, snappy accessories and, of course, that plump panettone – has been honed over the centuries in the weaving mills of Lecco and the bakeries of Bergamo, and continues to attract visitors from around the world today.

Still, this isn't a city to rest on its laurels: Milan is forever innovating. The choice can be overwhelming but we've sifted through the gaudy and outdated and come up with the goods, from refined leather shoes and designer tableware to dangerously addictive chocolates from a 19th-century *pasticceria*. There are plenty of surprises too: few expect to check in at Malpensa with artisanal gin and vintage stationery. Our advice? Bring an extra suitcase.

01 Antonio Citterio cutlery by littala from La Rinascente *rinascente.it*
02 Ettore Sottsass pepper mill by Alessi *alessi.com*
03 Biscuits by Giovanni Cova & C *giovannicovaec.it*
04 Chocolates by Pasticceria Cova *covamilano.com*
05 Gli Aironi arborio rice from Eataly *eataly.com*
06 Coffee by Hodeidah *hodeidah.it*
07 Aldo Rossi espresso pot by Alessi *alessi.com*
08 Panificio Freddi sbrisolona from Al Cervelee' de Milan *+39 02 837 2218*
09 Dolci e Delizie panettone from I Panini della Befi *+39 02 7602 3321*
10 Acacia honey by Hodeidah *hodeidah.it*
11 Maruzzella canned tuna from Eat's *eatstore.it*
12 Chocolates and pistachio cream by Pasticceria Marchesi *pasticceriamarchesi.com*
13 Le Tamerici onion chutney from Salvini *drogheriasalvini.it*
14 Collivasone biscuits from Ronchetti *ronchettidolciumi.it*
15 Gin by The Botanical Club *thebotanicalclub.com*
16 Extraomnes beer from Rebelot *rebelotnavigli.com*
17 Il Calepino wine from Enoteca Grancini *+39 02 2940 0090*
18 Campari from Il Camparino *camparino.it*
19 Franciacorta Coupé by Monte Rossa from N'Ombra de Vin *nombradevin.it*
20 Wallets by Valextra *valextra.com*
21 Cella shaving cream from Preattoni *preattoni.it*
22 Shaving set by Barberino's *+39 02 8343 9447*
23 Home fragrance by Culti *culti.com*
24 Jacket by Boglioli *boglioli.it*
25 Umbrella by Francesco Maglia *ombrellimaglia.eu*
26 Briefcase by Serapian *serapian.com*
27 Shoes by Santoni *santonishoes.com*
28 Trainers by Date *date-sneakers.com*

29 Notepaper and vintage stationery by Fratelli Bonvini *bonvini1909.com*
30 Handbag by Serapian *serapian.com*
31 Glasses by Kaleos, Snob, Epos and Charlie Max from Foto Veneta Ottica *fotovenetaottica.com*
32 Enzo Mari calendar by Danese *danesemilano.com*

33 Perfume by Prada *prada.com*
34 Ceramic plate by Laboratorio Paravicini *paravicini.it*
35 *Sculptures by Arnaldo Pomodoro* by Ugo Mulas and Francesco Leonetti from Fondazione Arnaldo Pomodoro *fondazionearnaldopomodoro.it*
36 *Bob Noorda Design* by Moleskine *moleskine.com*

37 Placemat by Society Limonta *societylimonta.com*
38 Essentials case by Caruso *carusomenswear.com*
39 Tie by Al Bazar *albazarmilano.it*
40 Bigi tie from Gemelli *gemelli.it*
41 Restelli gloves from La Rinascente *rinascente.it*
42 Shirts by Ermenegildo Zegna *zegna.com*

10 essays
— Viewpoints on Milan

1
Altered images
The changing face of Milan
by John Foot,
historian

2
Get shirty
Adventures in tailoring
by Laura Rysman,
writer

3
Tall storeys
Milan's upwardly
mobile skyline
by David Plaisant,
Monocle

4
On your bike
Cycling and the city
by Francesco Franchi,
designer and journalist

5
Food for thought
The problem with
Milanese cuisine
by Josh Fehnert,
Monocle

6
Design of the times
Salone del Mobile
by Francesca Picchi,
writer

7
Liquid gold
The history of the 'navigli'
by Melkon Charchoglyan,
Monocle

8
Perfect fit
Italian fashion
by Massimo Alba,
fashion designer

9
Not such a grey area
Parkland projects
by Olivia Mull,
writer

10
Centre stage
Milan's premier theatre
by Beatrice Carmi,
Monocle

This is
fascinating!
Wouldn't
you agree?

ESSAY 01

Altered images
The changing face of Milan

Whether it's a home for creative endeavour, an outward-looking European cultural centre or the self-proclaimed moral capital of Italy, Milan has always been a city willing to adapt.

*by John Foot,
historian*

In the late 19th century, Milan claimed to be the moral capital of Italy. The argument: as a city of business, money, banking and exchange, Milan was where things were done and made, as opposed to Italy's political capital, Rome, where money was simply spent (and wasted).

The label stuck and it tells us a lot about the city. This is a place that never stands still, a dynamic melting pot for entrepreneurs, universities, technical skills, creativity and finance. Milan has never been one to rest on its laurels; it has constantly re-invented itself. It has never seen itself as a tourist city or a living museum like Florence, Venice or Rome but rather a powerhouse. Thus, Milan was the city that Pirelli chose for its huge factory complex that tapped into bicycle and car production from the 19th century onwards; it was the place where Campari was made, where Alfa Romeo located its main factory, where Lambrettas were produced, and where innovative designers and inventors trained new generations of engineers, architects and – later – fashion experts.

All of this meant that Milan was ideally placed to soak up the extraordinary opportunities offered by the economic boom of the 1950s and 1960s. Migrants flocked to the city from all over Italy, pouring out of trains every morning into the cavernous halls of Stazione Centrale. Anna Maria Ortese described the station at the time as a "port of work, bridge of necessity, estuary of simple blood". It's also where Luchino Visconti shot the famous opening scene of *Rocco e i Suoi Fratelli* (1960), his controversial film about migrants in Milan.

According to official figures, 105,448 people arrived in 1962 alone, and 400,000 residents migrated to the city in the subsequent 15 years. It was during this period that Italian design captured the imagination of the world and it was in Milan that designer-architects such as Vico Magistretti and Gio Ponti worked with businesses on beautiful and mass-produced furniture, which sold in a flash. In the 1960s it was also the football capital of the world, with two teams – Inter and AC Milan – vying for the title of Europe's best team, along with Real Madrid.

"Thrumming nightclubs drowned out the factory sirens and disused manufacturing plants became art galleries or plush offices"

This was a city that was always open to outsiders: as well as being willing and able to absorb immigrants for building work, it was a welcoming home for writers, photographers and film-makers. As the boom came to its inevitable end, rather than wallowing in the past the city rebuilt itself yet again. In the 1980s the fashion designers who would dominate the industry for the next 30 years emerged here: Armani, Versace,

**Key dates in
Milan's history**
——
01 222BC
Conquered by the Romans.
02 1386
Construction of the
Duomo begins.
03 1861
Freed from the Austrians,
Milan joins a unified
Kingdom of Italy.

Dolce & Gabbana and Prada all came to call Milan home.

Factories closed but Milan never stopped moving forwards. The well-heeled Fashion Week crowds replaced the streams of workers, thrumming nightclubs drowned out the factory sirens and disused manufacturing plants became art galleries or plush offices.

Milan's post-industrial appearance was accompanied by political change, as new leaders used the city as a springboard to attain national power. The first to do so was Bettino Craxi, a Socialist who launched a new, moderate, left-wing platform and embraced fashion and television as a modern form of politics. His great friend Silvio Berlusconi was born and bred in Milan and would take up Craxi's mantle in the 1990s to rise to national power and fame.

But it was around this time that the label of "moral capital" began to lose its lustre. Both Craxi and Berlusconi were caught up in numerous corruption scandals, and successive judicial enquiries uncovered a web of illegal connections and finance that ran below the glittering surface of the city.

Milan's reputation took a hit yet, once again, the city rose from the ashes. A string of proactive mayors helped Milan rebrand itself as a tourist city, open to holidaymakers for the first time, while holding on to its traditional centres of excellence in banking and innovation. The city's Salone del Mobile became one of the hottest dates in the international calendar – even beyond the design crowd. The Expo in 2015 led to vast improvements in the city's infrastructure, as new museums and the Fondazione Prada flung open their doors. Milan now has four underground lines, with another on the way, and a hyper-efficient transport system. Leading architects have redrawn its skyline, making the city almost unrecognisable in recent years.

Today, Milan has numerous universities, numerous art centres and galleries, a whole central area dominated by fashion outlets, and an incredible urban park that incorporates old factories, bridges, allotments and architectural features. It even has a building called the Bosco Verticale (*see page 104*), designed by Stefano Boeri, where all apartments have real trees on the balconies, kept alive by a complicated and sustainable irrigation system.

While other destinations in Italy have stagnated, turning their gaze inwards, Milan has forged ahead, looking out towards Europe and the rest of the world. As the activist and local historian Primo Moroni once said, Milan is "a city that has eaten itself up many times and has in this way never become old". — (M)

ABOUT THE WRITER: John Foot is professor of modern Italian history at the University of Bristol. His works include *Milan since the Miracle: City, Culture and Identity* and *Calcio: A History of Italian Football*.

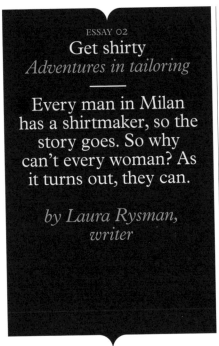

ESSAY 02
Get shirty
Adventures in tailoring

———

Every man in Milan has a shirtmaker, so the story goes. So why can't every woman? As it turns out, they can.

by Laura Rysman, writer

I've wanted to dress like a Milanese man ever since moving to Italy's most sophisticated city. Cross-dressing per se doesn't interest me but after a couple of years in Paris, where the nonchalant elegance of the local women struck me dumb, I couldn't help but notice that here, it's the men who have the starring role.

The men of Milan fascinate, regardless of age or beauty. For every young buck in a slim blazer there is a post-retirement fellow convincingly sporting a feathered fedora. They're dapper, not trendy, dressed nearly universally in variations on a suit, sockless Oxfords, a well-turned hat or man purse, and a rogue touch of colour. And they seem so at ease, like their clothes were made for them. Probably because they were.

Italy was slow to catch on to ready-to-wear fashion. As late as the 1950s, there were almost no boutiques. There were instead tailors, seamstresses and fabric shops. There was a heritage of high craftsmanship, dating back to the renaissance, and fine sartorial suiting. The 1960s introduced Italians to prêt-à-porter but the made-to-measure habit remained. That's the real secret of the soigné Milanese men I saw, a secret I could copy with help from some custom clothiers.

I'm a small fry, always needing shop-bought clothes to be taken in and hemmed, but in Milan I was surrounded by skilled hands who could measure and sew clothes for my half-pint frame. Every man in Milan has a shirtmaker, a friend said when I noted the embroidered initials on his cuff, and I vowed I would have a shirtmaker, too, and shirts with my initials.

I began humbly, with Camiceria Olga on Via Comelico, in business since 1948. It's the workhorse of Milanese shirtmakers, churning out high volumes to maintain the city's lowest prices, but with accommodating staff. Customers usually choose traditional shirting in plains and pinstripes but I brought my own raw silk, satin, even cashmere – trickier to sew – and they always said, yes, turning out perfectly fitted tops without complaint. "We try to satisfy even the craziest requests," said owner Ciro Verratti, with only a slightly pointed look in my direction.

Now I've moved on to some of Milan's newer shopfronts. Eligo on Corso Venezia, near Montenapoleone, is a narrow, elegant emporium that imbues you with a fabulous sensation of being a Quadrilatero della Moda kind of man (or woman – though it seems I am almost the only one to come here). Schedule an appointment with its sartorialist and you'll be tastefully guided through customising every detail of a shirt – and all aspects can be hand-sewn for a finer finish. The client's body is measured, fabric is carefully considered, then the order is sent to Naples or Puglia for the tailoring.

At Bespoke Milano on Via Achille Maiocchi, owner Francesca Fusi chats at length with customers to tease out their ideal shirt. She patiently talks to clients about their favourite colours, the most appropriate materials for a style and adds a few personal flourishes. When she

> "*We try to satisfy even the craziest requests,' says owner Ciro Verratti with only a slightly pointed look in my direction*"

Traditional Milan shirtmakers

01 Siniscalchi Camicie su Misura
siniscalchicamiciesumisura.com
02 Prata & Mastrale Sartoria Ambrosiana
pratamastrale.it
03 Camiceria Ambrosiana
camiceriaambrosiana.com

steers me towards an indigo linen over a certain beige to better flatter my skin tone, I'm thrilled – it's the kind of personal care I always imagined would take place in these made-to-measure domains.

Vestiges of Milan's more traditional (and more costly) shirtmakers remain, their workshops still busy with orders from the city's sharply dressed men, but for now I'm content with the row of bantam-sized, monogrammed shirts in my closet. Italian culture makes a lot of room for men – too much, I would venture – but after years of living in this country and trying to become more like the locals, I'm starting to understand how to move in on their territory, dressed for the part. — (M)

ABOUT THE WRITER: Splitting her time between citified reality in Milan and a dream life in Tuscany, Laura Rysman covers stories in Italy about fashion, design, travel and more as a contributor for MONOCLE, *The New York Times* and *T Magazine*.

ESSAY 03

Tall storeys
*Milan's upwardly
mobile skyline*

—

Recent years have
seen Milan's urban
development embrace
the skyscraper. But is it
genuine modernisation
or simply pandering to
big-name architects?

*by David Plaisant,
Monocle*

While accustomed to gleaming
high-rises in London, New York,
Bangkok and Hong Kong, the
recent sprouting of tall buildings
in Milan came as a surprise. Why
so? Living in Italy I am not so
naive as to indulge the vision that
the Italian urban skyline is all
terracotta rooftops and renaissance
balustrades. However, the sheer
quantity of vertiginous projects
that have, particularly in the past
15 years, pierced the Lombard
capital's landscape is startling.
Porta Nuova and the more
recent Tre Torri/CityLife are
headline clusters but all across
the city Milan is increasingly
building upwards. That Milan's
Manhattanisation startles me may

be because I live in Rome. Milan
is building as Rome continues to
crumble. While Milan's 2015 Expo
spurred a furious appetite to go
big and tall, the Italian capital's
development is glacial.

Milan's Second Miracle
(the first was in the Miracolo
Economico years of the 1950s
and 1960s) may not be at the cost
of the rest of the country but its
new towers – curved, spired or
tree-covered – are certainly
showing up the rest of Italy. And
as the Italian term *campanilismo*
(civic pride that stems from *il
campanile*, or the bell tower)
suggests, Milan is keeping a
tradition alive, except it's using
glass towers rather than stone
turrets and
domes.

*"Now, more
than ever,
Milan is
showing its
knack for
discreet elegance
matched with a
showy globalised
modernity"*

"The
skyscraper has
transformed
the life of the
Milanese,"
wrote Alberto
Savinio,
perhaps with a
little bemusement of the building
boom that Milan was experiencing
in the 1950s. The artist, journalist
and brother of metaphysical
painter Giorgio de Chirico went
on to speak of the mysterious
world that exists in these "vertical
cities" while the old "horizontal"
city went on, "blissfully stuck to
the plain with its low blocks and
closed gardens." Reading that
today, the contrast between the

**Architectural
highpoints**
—

01 Torre Velasca
Milan meets Gotham in
this 1950s skyscraper.
02 Pirelli Tower
A full 32 storeys of modernist
Milanese perfection.
03 Generali Tower
Zaha Hadid's tower, also known
as Lo Storto.

city of semi-secret renaissance and baroque courtyards and projects such as Stefano Boeri's 2014 Bosco Verticale (Vertical Forest) remains unchanged.

Now, more than ever, Milan is showing its knack for discreet elegance matched with a showy globalised modernity. And it's worth recalling the modernist dawn that Savinio described because it's still hard to miss. Gio Ponti and Pier Luigi Nervi's 1955 Pirelli Tower is as miraculous now as when it shot up, rising above the pollution-stained 19th-century buildings around it. Like cut crystal, it shows the Milanese willingness to impress, rendering beauty from high-quality materials.

After a lull in the three decades before the Millennium, Milan's skyline restarted its crystalline metamorphosis. At Porta Nuova, César Pelli's 2011 UniCredit Tower spirals upward with a confidence and preponderance that we have come to associate with Dubai or Shanghai. However, Italy's tallest building complements rather than competes with the iconic spires

of the Duomo, whose diminutive, golden Madonnina statue was once sanctified as symbolising the city's upper-height restriction. That unwritten limit was surpassed back in the 1950s with the construction of the Torre Breda on Piazza della Repubblica, at the time the business hub of the city. Even the Breda's modest 30 storeys exude a boldness and slender modernist determination that we can now call Milanese in spirit.

When it comes to building tall, straight lines and severity are not the order of the day in Milan. The city rebels as much as it conforms (when it comes to design at least) and today BBPR's Torre Velasca stands as an anomaly. Built between 1951 and 1958, it resolutely references the city's urban environment rather than the international (read: US) influences so popular at the time. Here, architect Ernesto Nathan Rogers and his team crafted a skyscraper like no other, where structure, materials (crushed terracotta, grit and marble) and historicism inform the façade, rather than fashionable norms obsessed with minimalism. Gio Ponti was an admirer for one, showing Milanese civic pride when he exalted the remarkable structure. "I admire, indeed I love, the Velasca Tower. I rejoice that this architectural form appeared in Milan and in no other city," he wrote in *Domus* magazine (which he founded).

At the CityLife development, which occupies the former site of the Fiera Milano (moved to vast new upgraded premises designed by Massimiliano Fuksas), Milan's latest vertiginous venture is quickly taking shape. The central showpiece is a cluster of three towers (including Zaha Hadid's twisting Generali Tower and Arata Isozaki's Allianz Tower) with their own new metro station, Tre Torri, on the gleaming Line 5.

It seems that the city's preoccupation with building tall has reached sky-high levels although there are those who pour scorn on this, labelling it a facile attempt to engage big-name architects (Daniel Libeskind has designed the third CityLife tower). Has Milan's upward building become more vanity project than considered urban construction? Perhaps. But like so much in the visual history of this most aesthetically conscious of cities, good presentation (what Italians call *bella figura*) is no after-thought. Milan's skyline, like the intricately sewn collar of a shirt or hem of a skirt, is being constantly designed. And for many a visitor, including this one, the results can be rather ravishing. — (M)

ABOUT THE WRITER: David Plaisant is MONOCLE's Rome correspondent and is regularly seen boarding a Frecciarossa high-speed train to report on stories from Trieste, Taranto and beyond.

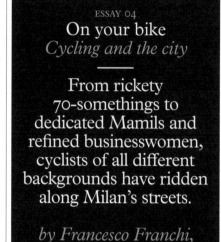

ESSAY 04
On your bike
Cycling and the city
────

From rickety 70-somethings to dedicated Mamils and refined businesswomen, cyclists of all different backgrounds have ridden along Milan's streets.

by Francesco Franchi, designer and journalist

Italy and cycling go hand in hand. The country has impressive form when it comes to producing international champions and bike brands and, while many places across the peninsula may claim to be its spiritual homeland, the sport's beating heart remains irrefutably in Milan.

Since the dawn of the two-wheeled era, countless bike manufacturers have chosen the city as their home: Colnago, Bianchi, De Rosa, Cinelli and Stelbel, to name a few. Every March the Milano Sanremo race opens the cycling season, which runs until the Giro di Lombardia in October. When it was inaugurated in 1905, the tour started and finished in Milan; it has since begun rotating between other towns in the region but occasionally still returns to the city before winding through the mountains around Lake Como.

Then there's the Giro d'Italia: the "pink race". The first departed from Milan's Piazzale Loreto at about 03.00 on 13 May 1909 in front of enthusiastic crowds, who turned up in their droves despite the early hour. As the 127 racers started out on their 400km journey down the muddy roads to Bologna, it soon became obvious that the race would be a success.

For a long time the inner-city Milanese cyclist was a rare beast; most commonly spotted on a Sunday, often pushing 70 years old, hunched over double and travelling at a snail's pace. He would be easily recognisable in his tight, bright onesie bearing the Mapei logo: the main sponsor in the heyday of 1980s cycling. His natural habitat would be the car-choked roads leading out of the city, to the north towards the lakes and to the south all the way to Pavia.

Until recently, Milan was crippled by traffic problems and famous for its smog; in the 2000s the city boasted the second-highest car ownership rate in Europe (after Rome) and only a handful of dedicated cyclists would bother tackling the architectural obstacles and often inclement weather of the city centre.

The 2008 introduction of a congestion charge for vehicles wishing to access the historical centre not only improved air quality but made the urban environment more welcoming for those on two wheels, kick-starting a renewed interest in cycling in the city. With it, new and varied species of cyclists started appearing on the streets.

In the beginning it was the hipsters with their fixed-gear bikes, bushy beards, tattoos and turned-up trouser hems. Next, the pedalling pensioners were joined by the "Mamil" (middle-aged man in Lycra) brigade: 40-somethings with chiselled calves and expensive technical-wear, riding professional carbon-fibre bikes that they

"For a long time the inner-city Milanese cyclist was a rare beast; most commonly spotted on a Sunday, often pushing 70 years old, hunched over double and travelling at a snail's pace"

religiously attend to and keep in their bedrooms. Mamils cover thousands of kilometres a year and make recurring pilgrimages to the cyclist's chapel, the Sanctuary of the Madonna of Ghisallo: a pass 754 metres above Lake Como, 70km from Milan.

Businesswomen also took to their bikes in serious numbers for

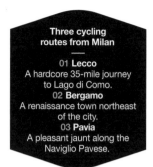

**Three cycling
routes from Milan**
—
01 **Lecco**
A hardcore 35-mile journey
to Lago di Como.
02 **Bergamo**
A renaissance town northeast
of the city.
03 **Pavia**
A pleasant jaunt along the
Naviglio Pavese.

the first time. Today they can often be sighted traversing the city centre in their tailored suits, elegant and resolute across the irregular, cobbled streets as they steer with one hand and hold an umbrella high with the other. They wield their heavy (preferably white) steeds with no technical apparatus but a rattan basket or two.

The city's bike-sharing scheme – BikeMi – now counts some 60,000 subscribers, 280 stations and 4,650 yellow and red bicycles in its ranks, and has played a great role in changing the commuting habits of the Milanese. A growing network of cycling paths – now totalling about 215km – may not be continuous but it has nonetheless worked as an incentive to trade four wheels for two.

A substantial squad of urban cyclists now hangs out in the many specialist shops and cafés that have opened across the city in recent years. They attend readings of books dedicated to cycling, watch bike-related documentaries and screenings of races.

The main destination remains Upcycle (*see page 38*), a café with an old-school mechanics workshop atmosphere: there's a DIY bike-repair corner, as well as food served at long communal tables, and a commendable selection of craft beer.

For your wine fix head to Ciclosfuso, a wine bar-cum-bistro and bike shop that hosts exhibitions, meet-ups and events (just don't go overboard on the *vino bianco*). If you're as passionate about flowers as bikes, Bici&Radici is the place for advice, knick-knacks and manuals.

A proper cycling culture has taken root in Milan: it's something to be proud of and not only because of its environmental credentials. Bikes are no longer simply convenient. As well as being a quick and easy way in which to move around the city, they look good. It's a revolution – and one that's most fitting of a design capital. — (M)

ABOUT THE WRITER: Francesco Franchi is the managing editor of *La Repubblica*, author of *Designing News* and co-author of *The Intelligent Lifestyle Magazine*.

ESSAY 05

Food for thought
The problem with Milanese cuisine

For chefs in Milan, experimentation and innovation are always on the menu. The problem is all that tinkering can leave a bad taste in your mouth.

by Josh Fehnert, Monocle

Don't let the French fool you or the Japanese jump on the bandwagon: the Italians are, on balance, right to insist that their food is the best in the world, it just is. What's more, the principles of picking fresh produce, passing down recipes and keeping dishes deliciously simple are some that the rest of the food world could learn from.

There's a caveat, though: visitors should be careful when picking a restaurant in Milan. This is a city where (more than elsewhere, I'd argue) the unbridled invention of chefs is prone to leaving diners hungry for something a little more tried-and-tested.

Although no more prevalent than in other cities, bad food in Milan is worse than anywhere else. A quick canvass of my editorial colleagues revealed that I wasn't alone in my observation about the drastically varying quality of the cuisine. No sooner had I asked than I was flooded with torrid tales of sea-urchin ice cream, sub-par sushi, hokey gimmicks and woefully over-thought entrées. Everyone I asked spoke of high expectations, warm smiles and solicitous service (the skills that most Italians seem to be born with) but food that either hit the mark squarely or missed it by a mile. This is a city of culinary extremes.

"Although no more prevalent than in other cities, bad food in Milan is worse than anywhere else"

Perhaps this polarity stems from the Milanese chefs' temptation to flaunt cutting-edge victuals to visiting fashion folk and design-minded trade-fair attendees. Whatever the cause, a rash of restaurants (some with top billings in the local press) are – without wishing to over-egg the point – disappointing indeed.

Now Milanese food isn't necessarily the kind of fodder you'll find in other Italian restaurants abroad. Crisp pizzas are more par for the course in Naples than the north, while

**Three rustic
Lombard dishes**
—
01 'Riso in cagnone'
Rice cooked with butter,
sage and parmesan.
02 'Tortelli di zucca'
This pumpkin ravioli has been
a favourite for centuries.
03 'Pan de mej'
Sweet corn bread, traditionally
a peasant snack.

pesto with crunchy pine nuts
hails from Liguria, and Piedmont
is the place for fresh pasta.
Remember that, despite its long
history, Italy as we know it has
only been a nation for the past
150 years or so and that, to make
sense of the country, you need
to understand the areas that
constitute it.

Regional delicacies have
developed over lifetimes. The
stolid mountain folk of Lombardy
(of which Milan is the capital)
favoured rough-and-ready risotto
dishes, polenta with cheese and
sausage, puffy panettone, and
ossobuco (crosscut veal shanks
braised with a vegetable-based
sauce). Milan's cooler climes
and reputation for tough work –
the Milanese are still known for
having this industrious streak
today – meant that local dishes
tended to sacrifice delicacy
and finesse in favour of heft; you
need to be full to work. Perhaps
it's that perceived rusticity of
the native nosh that chefs find
unbecoming of this most worldly
of Italian cities.

Milan is a cosmopolitan place
all right but one, I'd argue, that
excels when it can just be itself
– historic, lively, unpredictable,
intense and passionate – because
unfortunately the city is dreadful
at pretending to be other things.
Dishes, decor, chefs and
restaurants that defy what the
city has always done best and
overreach themselves tend to
look all the poorer in contrast
to the classics.

So what's the takeaway? Well,
stick to our tried-and-tested
restaurant run-down for starters,
of course. Then sideline the sushi,
the Michelin stars, the pomp
and the pretence, and treat with
caution the restaurants about
which the papers are raving.
For a taste of what's best about
Milanese food, grab some friends,
take up a table at an unpretentious
trattoria, sink a bottle of red
from somewhere in the path
of the Po River and order the
ossobuco. — (M)

ABOUT THE WRITER: Josh Fehnert is MONOCLE's food
and travel editor – and a regular visitor to Milan for
work and play. He's also the editor of *The Monocle
Guide to Drinking & Dining.*

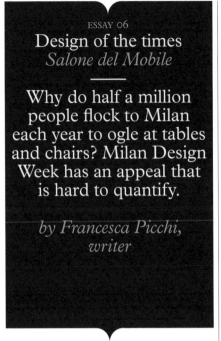

ESSAY 06

Design of the times
Salone del Mobile

Why do half a million people flock to Milan each year to ogle at tables and chairs? Milan Design Week has an appeal that is hard to quantify.

by Francesca Picchi, writer

Have you ever found yourself walking through kilometres of living rooms, dining rooms and kitchens; a surreal and endless parade of spotless tables, chairs and sofas, all engineered to offer ineffable domestic bliss? It may sound like a flight of fancy – or perhaps your worst nightmare, depending on how you feel about furniture – but such a fantasy world exists.

Each spring the Salone del Mobile rolls into town. On paper, it's no more than a glorified trade fair for industry specialists; in reality, it's an exuberant and indecipherable phenomenon that has no equal.

This flashmob of creativity transforms the city for a week and then disappears without trace. And rather than the closed doors and often intimidating air of Fashion Week, Salone is egalitarian and mostly open to all.

For that reason it's hard to monitor exactly how many people attend. Some place the figure at half a million (to put things in perspective, Milan's permanent population sits at about a million and a half), forming a mini city within the city.

So what attracts these throngs each April? Surely they aren't all here for the tables, chairs and sofas? Perhaps the answer is to be found not in the furniture but in the social aspect of the event – the way in which it brings together people and ideas.

It's not just the purpose-built exhibition halls, which hold some 2,000 exhibitors from 165 countries, that welcome exploration but also the city's nooks and crannies: the domain of the Fuorisalone (literally, "beyond Salone"). Each year, myriad activities and events sprout up in tucked-away corners that many Milanese don't even know about. Milan is an introverted city of hidden gardens and secret courtyards concealed behind imposing doors and forgettable façades but, thanks to the Fuorisalone, these intimate spaces are transformed into stages. And so the Salone gives the Milanese a chance to become tourists in their own city. Beyond the most organised neighbourhoods or "design districts" of Brera, Tortona, Cinque Vie, Via Durini and Ventura Lambrate, the city blossoms with independent initiatives.

However you define it, there's no denying that Salone is a voracious beast that feeds on lavish parties, lunches, dinners, aperitivos and cocktails. The Chamber of Commerce of Monza and Brianza estimates that some €20m is spent each year on such conviviality.

This sensory overload – the excess, the lack of order – is at the heart of Salone. The most eagerly anticipated billing in the most extraordinary premises can turn out to be the biggest flop, while unassuming events can end up being defining moments and taste-makers.

> *"This sensory overload – the hyper-stimulation, the excess, the unpredictability, the lack of certainty and order – is at the heart of Salone"*

Such was the case with Droog Design in the 1990s, when an unknown gallery presented a collection of its conceptual furniture and, in one evening, turned convention on its head. Rather than a standard chest of drawers, Droog haphazardly piled a few drawers on top of one another and bundled them

A history of Salone del Mobile
—

01 **1961**
The innaugural year.
02 **1976**
Salone launches the biennial Euroluce lighting fair.
03 **2005**
The fairground moves to its current site in Rho.

up with a strap. Instead of a regular lampshade, it slipped a few lightbulbs into some hazy milk bottles.

Something similar, and much more disruptive, happened with the emergence of Memphis in 1981. Ettore Sottsass (*see page 110*) brought a group of designers and entrepreneurs together to show their unconventional works in a shop behind the Piazza del Duomo. So many flocked to catch a glimpse of their bold, colourful and idiosyncratic designs that the road outside the showroom had to be closed to traffic.

Such occurrences are part of the charm of this event. Design has the power to communicate change and Salone provides the perfect mouthpiece. — (M)

ABOUT THE WRITER: Francesca Picchi is an architect, curator and journalist who lives and works in Milan. For 16 years she was on the editorial team at *Domus* magazine; today she splits her time between lecturing at ISIA in Florence and writing, thinking and dreaming about design.

ESSAY 07
Liquid gold
The history of the 'navigli'
———

With no river of its own, Milan once relied on a network of canals to provide it with a reliable source of water and mode of transport. Here's how the waterways might be making a comeback.

by Melkon Charchoglyan, Monocle

"I know how to move water from one place to another." These were the mystical words with which Leonardo da Vinci introduced himself to Ludovico Il Moro, the regent of Milan, in 1482.

Water was big business back then. Efficiently moving water from A to B promised abundant crops, healthy livestock and prosperity. The sound of crashing water was the jingle of the coin purse. Yet walking through Milan you'll notice that there is no river. In fact, the nearest major water source, the Ticino, lies some 30km west. While Italy's renaissance city-states drunk abundantly – Florence from the Arno, Venice from the Lagoon, Rome from the Tiber – dry-mouthed Milan simply stared at the scorching sun. But Milan has always been a city of "by hook or by crook". If it couldn't go to the river, the river would have to come to it.

The Naviglio Grande in the southwest, today lined with bars and restaurants, dates back to 1179. No one's quite sure who decided to dig the 50km canal but, when completed in 1257, it revolutionised the city. It connected Milan to Lake Maggiore in the northeast via the Ticino, allowing easy transportation of everything from grain to the pink Candoglia marble that was used to build the Duomo. And as well as going on to become financially lucrative (tolls and taxes for the use of the city's canals accounted for 4 per cent of government income by 1499) the *navigli* would also make for an excellent line of defence. This was something else that Milan needed, positioned so vulnerably near the northern border – although, as history proved, it wasn't always particularly effective.

Between 1435 and 1475, the dukes installed 90km of waterways throughout the city, forming a circle around what is now Milan's inner ring road. The intricate network was also navigable by ship thanks to 25 basins: open pools where vessels could manoeuvre. But the final flourish came courtesy of Leonardo, who applied his wits to the Naviglio Martesana. This canal ran from Lake Como to the outskirts of Milan but couldn't be connected to the inner network due to the uneven land.

"Not only would the 'navigli' be financially lucrative, they would also make for an excellent line of defence, something else Milan needed"

In the 1480s, after being commissioned by Ludovico Il Moro to design this last link, the polymath spent much time on the southern shores of Como, specifically near the river Fiumelatte. At just 250 metres long, it's one of the shortest rivers in Italy and dries up come October, only to return in a violent torrent in mid-March. Leonardo studied it for years, going deep into the caverns above in search of its source. He never did find it, and what lesson he took away from this miraculous river is a matter of contention, but his

Leonardo's ideas

01 Ornithopter
A pair of wings spanning more than 10 metres, made from silk.
02 Fighting vehicle
A cone-shaped early tank that could fire in any direction.
03 Scuba kit
A leather diving suit and mask for stealthy underwater attacks.

years of observation certainly informed his understanding of the movement and control of water. When designing the extension to the Naviglio Martesana, he introduced artificial cascades to slow the current (reminiscent of the cascades of the Fiumelatte) and efficient flood basins that could overcome the land's irregular topography. By 1497, you could sail uninterrupted from Lago di Como to the Mediterranean via Milan.

Over the next 500 years the *navigli* were Milan's main means of transport and saw much improvement; most memorable was Napoleon's installation of the Naviglio Pavese in 1805, which ran from Milan to the city of Pavia, 33km south. But all good things must come to an end. With the advent of the Industrial Revolution – and trains – the *navigli* lost importance. After all, who wants to travel at just 3km per hour? All that the canals were good for now was sinking corpses. Indeed, the putrefying smell and build-up of filth made certain stretches of water unbearable.

Little by little the government realised that the canals were redundant and would be better off supporting train tracks and cars. Most of the central *navigli* were paved over under the Fascist regime in the 1920s and 1930s. The last to say its farewell was Leonardo's stretch of the Naviglio Martesana in 1968.

But the government that oversaw their demise missed a crucial point. The *navigli* held a symbolic significance; they were beautiful (when well-maintained) and inseparable from the city's historic pride. And the Milanese never forgot about them: since the early 2000s, a strong movement has been brewing to reintroduce the canals. Orchestrated primarily by Giuseppe Sala, current mayor of Milan and CEO of the 2015 Expo, a petition to do so won 450,000 signatures in 2011 (that's a third of the city's population). And the first major step came in 2015, when the Darsena basin – the reservoir at the end of the Naviglio Grande – was transformed from a neglected wasteland into a pristine pool lined with promenades and bars.

Restoring the *navigli* isn't a Milanese delusion. The idea has the backing of architects such as Jacques Herzog (of architectural practice Herzog + de Meuron), who sees their potential for enriching the city's appearance, creating an environment for leisure and introducing a new transport network. It has had strong government support and the first 2km are slated to open by 2022.

Venice, Amsterdam, Hamburg and countless others enjoy their historic waterways, so why shouldn't Milan? Sure, Candoglia marble now flies by plane, and most canals serve only to transport wide-eyed tourists or look pretty on a summer's evening, but that's good enough for us – and most of Milan too. — (M)

ABOUT THE WRITER: Melkon Charchoglyan is a researcher at MONOCLE. He spent a lot of time drinking Aperol spritz on the Naviglio Grande – in the name of research, of course.

ESSAY 08
Perfect fit
Italian fashion

———

Renowned as the fashion capital of the world, Milan's mix of personal attention and cosmopolitan attitude makes it a cut above the rest.

by Massimo Alba, fashion designer

My career in fashion began in the mid-1980s, making cashmere knitwear for men and women, before I moved on to stints as creative director for labels such as Agnona, Ballantyne and Malo. Back then Milan was a different place and the fashion world as a whole was much simpler. The Italian industry revolved around two big names: Armani and Versace. There was no fast fashion, no pressure to design and sell around the clock, no offering new items every month and no pre-collections to boost sales.

The retail scene has changed a lot. In Italy you find many of the same shops and chains that you have in the likes of Amsterdam and Berlin – or even at the airport. Yet despite losing some multibrand neighbourhood retailers, Milan has seen boutiques and independent shops opening beyond the traditional shopping district of Quadrilatero della Moda. I opened my first Massimo Alba shop (*see page 61*) in the Brera district, on a quiet street that's now attracting increasing interest from shoppers and brands looking to reinvent themselves.

In my years working here I've witnessed Milan becoming a more vibrant, multicultural city; today it truly deserves its title as a fashion capital. Hop on the metro and you'll see faces from all over the world. The skyline has changed – we've embraced skyscrapers – and there's now a wonderful mix of architecture from different periods. Another significant change has been the arrival of the high-speed train network, which brings in shoppers from Bologna, Florence and Turin looking for something new. I'm happy to say that, alongside tourists, I get lots of Italians coming in for my clothes.

The balance between Milan's cosmopolitan make-up and historic city centre has given the city a wonderful spirit. That's why it's important to invest in physical retail: to bring people in, to give them a special experience and a sense of discovery; to show them what's unique about Milan. We need to move away from the cookie-cutter approach of more and more fashion chains and big brands that people can find anywhere in the world. Italy was never one to embrace the shopping-mall culture and I believe that it's important to stick to that, supporting the independent neighbourhood shops and giving visitors an encounter to remember.

I chose to open my shop in an area close to the Orto Botanico behind the Pinacoteca. I love nature – all the colours I use in my clothes are drawn from the natural world – so I papered the walls with pages from encyclopaedias and old gardening journals. I also kept the vintage shopkeeper's bell on the door so when people come in they hear a comforting ring that announces their arrival, something from a bygone era. I would like to return to a time when retail was more personal and removed from the data-driven game of online sales and e-commerce.

"It's important to invest in physical retail. To bring people in, to give them a special experience, a sense of discovery; to show them what's unique about Milan"

Although fashion is supposed to be about fast-changing trends and forever offering something new and exciting, I prefer not to

> **Milanese designers**
> ────
> **01 Mario Prada**
> The late founder of the renowned fashion house.
> **02 Franco Moschino**
> Remembered for his bold designs.
> **03 Stefano Gabbana**
> One half of the flamboyant duo behind the flashy eponymous label.

alter people's wardrobes every six months. Clothes shouldn't have an expiry date. I want to offer pieces that can be worn indefinitely. All of our items are washed after being constructed and dyed: we remove that rigid feel of unworn clothes and give them a natural finish. Comfort and touch are fundamental to what we do so everything we make is soft; we want our clothes to offer emotional comfort too. My collections mix the new with the old and nothing that I design is very loud – it's an ethos that suits Milan, especially of late. — (M)

ABOUT THE WRITER: After working behind the scenes in the Milanese fashion industry since the 1980s, Treviso native and knitwear maestro Massimo Alba launched his eponymous fashion label in 2006.

ESSAY 09

Not such a grey area
Parkland projects

———

Milan's traditional image of being grey and miserable is changing as the city goes green and bushy.

by Olivia Mull, writer

The picture painted of Milan is often monochrome: an industrial city with grey-stone architecture and smog-filled air. Even its status as Italy's economic and fashion capital conjures up images of black-clad residents in dark glasses. But the so-called grey city has always had greenery at its heart and is fast morphing into one of the most verdant cities in Europe.

The historic centre of Milan, which radiates from the Duomo, is dotted with green enclaves. Hidden behind high walls and austere façades are ancient gardens and courtyards that were once the private world of churches, monasteries and palazzos.

Walking down the super-narrow Via Cappuccio, you can glimpse these pockets of greenery through curved arches. Perhaps the most spectacular is at number seven: a plant-filled, 15th-century cloister. During the Salone del Mobile, attention-seeking installations often occupy the best of these courtyards, including Policlinico of Milan's Cortile della Farmacia and Università degli Studi di Milano's Cortile del Settecento.

Some of the most recent architecture projects in the city make visible the private green spaces of Milan's past. The Bosco Verticale skyscrapers (*see page 104*) flaunt hectares-worth of trees on their cantilevered balconies. These not only camouflage the architecture but also absorb CO_2, release oxygen and cool the environment.

Stefano Boeri, the project's architect, describes Bosco Verticale as the mother of a new wave of greenery because the Milanese – like many city-dwellers – have become obsessed with urban gardening, filling their balconies with colourful plants, tumbling succulents and fragrant herbs. Brera is one of the areas most densely filled, with leafy

"The so-called grey city has always had greenery at its heart and is fast morphing into one of the most verdant cities in Europe"

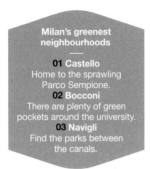

**Milan's greenest
neighbourhoods**
———
01 Castello
Home to the sprawling
Parco Sempione.
02 Bocconi
There are plenty of green
pockets around the university.
03 Navigli
Find the parks between
the canals.

balconies and rooftops; at its heart is the *Orto fra i Cortili*, a rooftop urban vegetable garden that's typical of many in the city.

Even with a history of such private green spaces, Milan can boast one of Europe's most ancient public parks, the Giardini Pubblici. When it opened at the end of the 18th century, it made greenery something for everybody, not just the rich. For decades, this and the slightly younger Parco Sempione were the two biggest green spaces in Milan.

At the end of the 1900s three parks were established on the outskirts of the city, effectively wrapping it in a green blanket: Parco Nord Milano in the north, which combined derelict industrial areas, an old airport and unkempt meadows into a park; the Parco Agricolo Sud Milano agricultural land in the south; and Boscoincittà, a wood in the northwest. Many other projects follow this vein of High Line-style change, including the Porta Romana railway yard that surrounds OMA's Fondazione Prada (*see page 103*).

Since the new millennium, even more parks have appeared and recreational green spaces are emerging as part of fledgling residential projects. Recent additions include the parkland around the CityLife towers (*see page 105*) and the Biblioteca degli Alberi (Library of Trees) in Isola.

From a bird's-eye view all of the above may seem disconnected. Over recent years, however, many projects have been proposed that weave these emerald enclaves together: some are underway, others are proposals (and all have similar names). Land Studio's Green Rays wants to create eight tree-lined routes connecting the central parks to the greenery in the outskirts, passing through the lush spaces of new developments along the way. Meanwhile, Boeri's Green River aims to collate seven disused railway yards and turn them into public parks, forests, orchards and a network of bicycle paths. Both follow in the footsteps of the Parco Orbitale project, which launched in 2004.

These joined-up green projects are offering the city a lifeline by absorbing CO_2 and producing oxygen. Milan is certainly a city that is securing itself a green future, filled with fresh air and happy residents. — (M)

ABOUT THE WRITER: Olivia Mull is managing editor of online architecture and design magazine *Dezeen*. Originally from the Fens, London is now her base but she wishes it were Italy.

Centre stage
Milan's premier theatre

With a storied history and a glorious line-up of past performances, the Teatro alla Scala is one of Italy's – and perhaps the world's – most celebrated cultural institutions.

*by Beatrice Carmi,
Monocle*

"In the 18th century, a trip to the theatre meant far more than just music and ballet"

Milan's Teatro alla Scala was born from the ashes – although not its own. In 1776 a devastating fire raged through the city's Regio Ducale theatre, razing it to the ground and leaving the Milanese theatre-less. At the time, Milan – then a dukedom known as the Ducato di Milano – was under the rule of the Austrian Habsburgs, who were generally regarded as a relatively enlightened bunch. Archduchess Maria Theresa, the ruler of the day, surrounded herself with a bevy of intellectuals and philosophers and was responsible for initiating many cultural reforms that made Milan one of the most receptive cities in Europe.

It was Maria Theresa who indulged the citizens' plea for a new theatre, commissioning architect Giuseppe Piermarini to design it. Rather than building it on the grounds of the old one next to the Palazzo Reale, a new site was chosen on the ruins of the 14th-century church of Santa Maria della Scala – which would give the theatre its name.

In less than two years, under Piermarini's direction, the Milanese built what 19th-century French writer Stendhal described as "the most beautiful theatre in the world" and on 3 August 1778 the new venue threw open its doors to a staging of Antonio Salieri's opera *Europa Riconosciuta*.

In the 18th century, a trip to the theatre meant far more than just music and ballet. The city's most glamorous rendezvous point, La Scala hosted everything from lavish feasts to business meetings, private parties and even gambling under its roof, all to the sound of live music. The theatre's boxes were owned and rented by the city's richest families and were used as an extension of their private homes; the proprietors would decorate them according to their own tastes and were responsible for taking care of the lighting and heating.

La Scala soon became a pivotal cultural institution and went on to assume an important role in Italy's unification – *il Risorgimento* – which saw Italy's motley collection of realms and dukedoms become a single country in 1861. The unifying process was long and troubled and music itself had a helping hand.

In 1842 another Giuseppe – Verdi, perhaps Italy's most renowned composer – played his part in proceedings when his *Nabucco* opera was first performed at La Scala. Recounting the plight of the Jews as they were conquered and exiled from their motherland by the Babylonians, *Nabucco* includes the well-known chorus "Va' Pensiero", a melancholic but rousing chant that the Jews sing about their "beautiful and lost homeland".

At a time when the Italian peninsula was itself subjected to Austrian rule, the chorus was immediately interpreted as a metaphor for the country's situation and appropriated a renewed political slant. From that moment on, Verdi became a symbol of *il Risorgimento*'s cause and legend has it that during the final years of the Austrian occupation, the words "Viva Verdi" – which were scrawled across the city's walls – were in fact an acronym for "Viva Vittorio Emanuele Re d'Italia" (Long live Vittorio Emanuele, king of Italy).

"It is by far the theatre with the greatest tradition in the world," says La Scala's CEO and artistic director Alexander Pereira. "Many of the greatest operas ever composed were first staged here." And while some might find such a glorious past a burdensome inheritance, Pereira is not one to be easily daunted: La Scala recently expanded its annual production calendar and strives to stage more operas than ever. "Opera is a very complete form of art that shows an interaction between music, words and scenery. It's incredibly expensive to produce but also fascinating," says Pereira. "Think of the 'Mona Lisa': we wouldn't throw it away because the insurance is too expensive, would we?" — (M)

Operas that premiered at La Scala

—

01 **'Norma', 1831**
Vincenzo Bellini's portrayal of a strong priestess.
02 **'Andrea Chénier', 1896**
Featuring the famous aria "La Mamma Morta".
03 **'Madama Butterfly', 1904**
Giacomo Puccini's beautiful but tragic love story.

ABOUT THE WRITER: Beatrice Carmi is a researcher at MONOCLE. She studied opera in Milan and loves Russian literature more than anything (her husband understands).

Culture
—— The art of the city

The cultural life of many Italian cities is dominated – sometimes overwhelmingly – by historical ruins and big-name museums with lengthy queues. Milan's, on the other hand, is played out on a slightly smaller scale and all the better for it.

Manageable and with a sense of discovery about them, the city's cultural heavyweights tend to maintain a modest profile (except for the inimitable Duomo, of course). Indeed, Milan's greatest galleries and most fascinating designers' studios are often hidden away at the back of a courtyard or on the upper floors of a well-to-do apartment block.

A wealth of post-industrial spaces and a farsighted, experimental approach have meant that there's plenty to seek out on the city's fringes, too: from Fondazione Prada to Pirelli HangarBicocca, contemporary art has found a place to take root here and flourish.

①
Pinacoteca di Brera, Brera
Italian masterworks

The huge statue of Napoleon in the courtyard hints to this museum's past: in 1809 the French emperor exhibited Italian art looted by his armies in the 17th-century palazzo. Today it holds the pick of Italy's masters, including Raphael and Caravaggio, and modern works by Umberto Boccioni and Modigliani.

Careful lighting and fresh decor, courtesy of new director James Bradburne, make the canvases an even greater pleasure to see. Visit the Ettore Sottsass-designed glass restoration chamber to see paintings unframed for retouching.
28 Via Brera, 20121
+ 39 02 7226 3264
pinacotecabrera.org

Ecclesiastical masterpieces

01 Basilica di Santa Maria delle Grazie, Magenta:
Leonardo da Vinci spent two decades in Milan and, among other great works, left behind one particularly famed renaissance fresco: "The Last Supper". Its unorthodox oil-based medium hasn't quite stood the test of time (it was completed in 1498) but getting advance tickets to see it for just 15 minutes is an extraordinary and unmissable experience.
legraziemilano.it

02 Chiesa di San Maurizio al Monastero Maggiore, Sant'Ambrogio: This sanctuary of a former Benedictine convent, dating back to 1503, is covered with a jaw-dropping collection of gilded, richly hued paintings and frescos. Sometimes referred to as the Sistine Chapel of Milan, it effectively represents Leonardo's contemporaries, especially Bernardino Luini.
15 Corso Magenta, 20123

03 Chiesa di Santa Maria presso San Satiro, Missori: This 15th-century church epitomises the appreciation for artistic perspective that arose in the renaissance. Donato Bramante painted one of the first examples of trompe l'oeil in the building's foreshortened apse to create the illusion of space. Gilt-embossed columns give off the impression that the area – which is in fact less than a metre deep – is far more expansive than it actually is.
17-19 Via Torino, 20123

Mudec, Tortona
Art and artefacts

The Museum of Cultures brings historical and social context to the exhibitions that it organises: shows that focus on the likes of Miró and Kandinsky, for example, tease out pleasantly unexpected angles to their work. Naturally, there's a vast display of artefacts from different ethnic traditions too, from utensils to musical instruments.

Inaugurated in 2015, the zinc-clad building has a sinuous, wonderfully luminous matte-glass hall inside, while on the second floor is fêted chef Enrico Bartolini's inventive two-star restaurant.
56 Via Tortona, 20144
+39 02 54 917
mudec.it

③
Gallerie d'Italia, Duomo
Creative deposits

When Intesa Sanpaolo transformed a 1911 neoclassical bank on Piazza della Scala into a museum to showcase the company's extensive art collection, they kept much of the original structure in place. A stroll through its stellar selection of modern art is marked by reminders of the business that built up such a stockpile: old teller windows, antique vault doors and intricate brass letterboxes are all interspersed amongst the paintings.

Though some foreign artists are present, it's the span of Italian works that's truly impressive, from 19th-century masters such as Antonio Canova and Francesco Hayez to representatives of every major art movement in Italy from the 20th century, including Lucio Fontana, Enrico Baj and Mario Merz.
6 Piazza della Scala, 20121
+39 800 167 619
gallerieditalia.com

④
Museo del Novecento, Duomo
Through the ages

The neo-Roman Palazzo dell'Arengario (*see page 113*) was completed in the 1950s by architects including Piero Portaluppi. Within one of its twin towers on the Piazza del Duomo you'll find this formative collection of Italian 20th-century art.

A journey through the museum is a steady, chronological rise from Pellizza da Volpedo's neo-impressionism to the Pollock-esque canvases of Tancredi Parmeggiani and Emilio Vedova. There are temporary exhibitions too, such as *New York New York*, a retrospective on Italian artists in the US.

Like a Dantean finish beneath the stars, your visit will culminate under Lucio Fontana's 1951 lasso-like neon installation in a gallery space with knockout views of the Duomo. If there's one museum to visit in Milan, it's this one.
1 Via Guglielmo Marconi, 20123
+39 02 8844 4061
museodelnovecento.org

⑤
Galleria d'Arte Moderna, Porta Venezia
Modern masterpieces

This museum – housed in an 18th-century palazzo by architect Leopoldo Pollack – charts the Milanese art scene beyond the neoclassical age, from the marble sculptures of Antonio Canova to the mid-20th century and the likes of futurist Giacomo Balla.

Among the 4,000 artworks held here are prized collections donated by the prominent Grassi and Vismara families, including pieces by Manet, Van Gogh and Picasso. After a tour, pop into Lù Bar: a Sicilian café in the east wing.
16 Via Palestro, 20121
+39 02 8844 5947
gam-milano.com

6

Triennale di Milano, Sempione
Design of the times

The Triennale di Milano started out as the modern palazzo that hosted Italy's decorative arts, industrial design and architecture triennial in 1933. Its aim is still to represent the whole scope of the design industry, "from spoon to city", and since 2007 it has been a permanent museum that showcases the history of Italian design.

The rich collection is displayed – always partially – across the upstairs floor, accessed by a suspended bridge. The theme-led displays often last for up to a year: recent topics have included women in design and modern-day robots in the kitchen. Plus, after a 20-year hiatus, the original triennale formula was reprised in 2016.

Pop out of the tall portico at the back and you'll find a cheerful sculpture garden featuring Giorgio de Chirico's "I Bagni Misteriosi".
6 Viale Emilio Alemagna, 20121
+ 39 02 724 341
triennale.org

⑦
Casa-Museo Boschi di Stefano,
Porta Venezia
Art house

The former home of husband-
and-wife art collectors Antonio
Boschi and Marieda di Stefano
can be found in a 1930s art deco
apartment block designed by
architect Piero Portaluppi. In
2003 it became a museum of their
modern Italian art collection, with
works dating from the early 20th
century to the 1950s (the 11 rooms
are organised in chronological
order). Apart from a table by
Portaluppi and a Bechstein piano,
all of the furniture has been
bought and arranged to reflect the
historical context of the pieces.

Despite the home being tightly
packed with art, there's only room
for 300 of the 2,000 works in the
collection, including masterpieces
by both Umberto Boccioni and
Carlo Carrà and still lives by
Giorgio Morandi.
15 Via Giorgio Jan, 20129
+39 02 7428 1000
fondazioneboschidistefano.it

By the book
—
In 1770, empress Maria
Theresa gave the Milanese the
Biblioteca Nazionale Braidense
to "cultivate their minds". It's
housed in the same building
as the Pinacoteca di Brera.
Anyone over the age of 16 can
access the reading room (just
remember your ID).
braidense.it

Home is where the art is

Milan has a clutch of sumptuous
dwellings donated by wealthy
patrons to become museums.
Here's our pick of the three
best *case museo* in the city.

01 **Museo Bagatti Valsecchi,
Quadrilatero della Moda:**
This was once home
to two brothers who,
in the 19th century,
remade the interiors in
the 16th-century Lombard
style. It opened its
collection of renaissance
art and objects to the
public in 1994.
museobagattivalsecchi.org

02 **Villa Necchi Campiglio,
Monforte:** This concrete
villa (*see page 111*) was
built in 1935 by Milan's
renowned modern
architect Piero Portaluppi.
Today it can be toured
(the original furniture is
still in place) but most
people choose to sit in
the tranquil poolside
garden and read.
visitfai.it/villanecchi

03 **Museo Poldi Pezzoli,
Quadrilatero della Moda:**
Opened in 1881 and filled
with precious works from
renaissance masters such
as Botticelli and Bellini,
this is the oldest of Milan's
case museo.
museopoldipezzoli.it

*It's been
hours since my
last supper*

❶
Assab One, Cimiano
Hot off the press

Inhabiting a former printing press,
Assab One presents installations
that are often enhanced (if not
overshadowed) by the exposed
concrete and raw floorings of the
vast factory space.

Curator Elena Quarestani (heir
of the owners of the publishing
plant) turned the business into a
cultural centre in 2004. Its aim is
to bring art to both aficionados
and the uninitiated, a goal that's
particularly relevant to the
underprivileged area around
nearby Via Padova. The gallery's
name is partly a tribute to the name
for an Eritrean port – a hint at the
director's hope to make this a place
for cross-cultural exchange.
1 Via Assab, 20132
+39 02 282 8546
assab-one.org

①
Monica de Cardenas,
Porta Garibaldi
Broad remit

Monica de Cardenas was educated in Switzerland – hence her gallery's two other locations in Lugano and Zuoz. This space was founded in 1992 to show photography but has widened its scope to include paintings, sculptures and drawings. You'll find established names such as Alex Katz alongside emerging artists including Rä di Martino.
4 Via Francesco Viganò, 20124
+ 39 02 2901 0068
monicadecardenas.com

Pirelli HangarBicocca, Bicocca
Vast display

Housed in a colossal former locomotive manufacturing plant (15,000 sq m with ceilings four storeys high), this non-profit art foundation is the permanent home of Anselm Kiefer's lofty towers "The Seven Heavenly Palaces". It exhibits solo shows by international contemporary artists, who often create site-specific works to fill the awe-inspiring space.

It may be a schlep from the city centre but this is Milan's most rewarding contemporary-art venue; the in-house bistro and bar make the journey even more worthwhile.
2 Via Chiese, 21026
+ 39 02 6611 1573
hangarbicocca.org

②
Fondazione Prada, Ripamonti
All that glitters

Prada's public gallery is worth every minute it takes to get there on the metro. Rem Koolhaas transformed a century-old distillery into an inimitable space (*see page 103*) that includes a gold-leaf gallery housing permanent installations by Robert Gober and Louise Bourgeois, plus exhibition halls, a cinema, a library and even a café designed by Wes Anderson (*see page 37*).

There are roughly six exhibitions a year but, if the current display isn't to your taste, pay the entrance fee anyway: the real masterpiece comes courtesy of Koolhaas.
2 Largo Isarco, 20139
+ 39 02 5666 2611
fondazioneprada.org

Love matters
—
Right in front of Milan's stock exchange on Piazza degli Affari is Maurizio Cattelan's statue of a middle finger. Known around the city as "The Finger", the official title is "Love" – an acronym for *libertà* (freedom), *odio* (hate), *vendetta* (revenge) and *eternità* (eternity).

2

Gió Marconi, Porta Venezia
Expert opinion

The anchor of the Porta Venezia art scene, Gió Marconi opened a fresh new space here in 2015, marking 25 years as one of Milan's most prominent gallerists.

Avant garde international talents mix with retrospectives of artists from the 1960s to the 1990s, the period when Marconi's father ran his own high-profile gallery. The father-and-son duo collaborated on an experimental art space from 1986 to 1990 but now Marconi has established himself independently as a guru of contemporary European and international art.
20 Via Alessandro Tadino, 20124
+ 39 02 29 404 373
giomarconi.com

3

Kaufmann Repetto, Porta Garibaldi
Youthful focus

Originally named solely after its first founder, Francesca Kaufmann, this gallery took on its current moniker in 2010, along with a new partner – Chiara Repetto – and venue.

The range of media includes photography and performance (with a penchant for video and installations) by younger artists, be they Italian or international, and features pieces by Nicola Martini and Eva Rothschild. The space, which was designed by architect Frank Boehm, also has a small front garden that's often used to host site-specific works.
7 Via di Porta Tenaglia, 20121
+ 39 02 7209 4331
kaufmannrepetto.com

4

Lia Rumma, Bullona
Respected authority

Neapolitan gallerist Lia Rumma has been a force in the nation's contemporary-art scene since the 1970s. Since 1999 she has operated a Milanese outpost, which moved to this four-level location – a stark white box designed by CLS Architetti – in 2010.

Rumma is credited as a vital player in the discovery of movements such as arte povera and land art, and has hosted artists from Andreas Gursky and Alberto Burri to Marina Abramovic. Her choice of emerging names is just as high-calibre.
19 Via Stilicone, 20154
+ 39 02 2900 0101
liarumma.it

⑤
Massimo de Carlo, Quadrilatero
della Moda & Lambrate
Twice as nice

For three decades, this gallery has
brought rising and established
international stars to Milan and
catapulted Italians onto the
international stage.

Its primary gallery in Lambrate
launched a second location in 2016
in the city's Palazzo Belgioioso.
Now visitors can enjoy works by
Ai Weiwei, Maurizio Cattelan,
and Alighiero Boetti in either a
historical context or the original
gallery's converted industrial space.
2 Piazza Belgioioso, 20121
+39 02 3663 6990;
5 Via Giovanni Ventura, 20134
+39 02 7000 3987
massimodecarlo.com

⑥
Zero, Risorgimento
Big ideas

Paolo Zani's gallery has a
reputation for being restless,
not only in its artistic curiosity
but also in its choice of locations.
Since first opening in 2000 in the
town of Piacenza, it moved to
Milan in 2003 and then hopped
between spots across Porta Venezia
and Lambrate before landing in
Risorgimento in 2014.

The entrance foyer may
suggest that the gallery space
amounts to next to nothing but
turn right and a long series of
rooms unfolds. The focus is on
works in all media that deal with
big themes such as what makes
us human (or what constitutes art
in the first place); young Italian
and international artists, including
Massimo Grimaldi and Neïl
Beloufa, are regular features.
46 Viale Premuda, 20129
+39 02 8723 4577
galleriazero.it

⑦
Six Gallery, Porta Genova
Cloistered but accessible

In 2017, architects Fanny
Bauer Grung and David Lopez
Quincoces, together with design
director Mauro Orlandelli, turned
a former monastery into a gallery
of furniture and design by mid-
century prodigies such as Gabriella
Crespi and Pierre Jeanneret.

"We have rare and iconic
designs, as well as anonymous
articles without the high price tag,"
says Grung. "It's one of Milan's
most accessible galleries." That
said, visits are by appointment only.
Once you've perused the gallery,
sample the flavours at adjoining
courtyard bistro Sixieme.
7 Via Scaldasole, 20123
six-gallery.com

Studios and archives
History in the making

①

Fondazione Achille Castiglioni, Castello
Design origins

This studio looks exactly the same as it did when Castiglioni occupied it. His dedicated relatives have opened up the rooms (by appointment only) and personally guide you through his prototypes, drawings and designs, which – in a welcome move away from museum-like fetishisation – visitors are welcome to touch, use and sit on.
27 Piazza Castello, 20121
+ 39 02 805 3606
fondazioneachillecastiglioni.it

②

Fondazione Studio Museo Vico Magistretti, Monforte
Designs on display

Designer Vico Magistretti's office feels more like a gallery than a musty relic. His last assistant, Paolo Imperatori, set up displays to show his master's drawings and projects, both in architecture and furniture: 3D models of his buildings are displayed alongside famed chair designs such as Selene and Silver.
    Changing exhibitions centre on Magistretti's designs and their influence, and there are also workshops for kids. The opening hours are odd though: visit only on Tuesday and Thursday afternoons.
20 Via Conservatorio, 20122
+ 39 02 7600 2964
vicomagistretti.it

③

Fondazione Franco Albini, Pagano
Local hero

Following Renzo Piano's 2007 Triennale retrospective of architect and designer Franco Albini, the Milanese government opened Albini's studio and archive to the public. "Albini's ethos was lightness; it was about reducing, not adding," says his son and the studio's lead architect Marco Albini. "The goal of the foundation is to help people understand this."
    Through pre-booked guided tours he discloses the history and ideas behind his father's designs, including the 1952 Fiorenza chair and 1940 Veliero bookshelf.
13 Via Bernardino Telesio, 20145
+ 39 02 498 2378
fondazionefrancoalbini.com

Main man

If you plan to visit the Via Dezza Apartments (*see page 110*) to see the architect Gio Ponti's work, check out his former studio on the ground floor (by appointment only). The Archivio Gio Ponti features photos and projects arranged by his daughter Lisa.
gioponti.org

Live venues
Stage coaching

Plugged in
Alfresco films come with headphones

① Mare Culturale Urbano, Trenno
Community theatre

This pale brick farmhouse from the 1600s reopened as a cultural centre in 2016. Located near the San Siro stadium, the restored structure hosts a stage in its courtyard for a packed roster of concerts, plays and films. Meanwhile, several communal tables in the restaurant/bar are designed to encourage people to linger.

"At a regular theatre, you come for two hours and leave without talking to anyone," says founder Andrea Capaldi. "Here we spend a lot of time together." The *mare* in the venue's name means "sea" – something that's otherwise lacking in Milan. "The sea is what has always brought people together to explore the world."
15 Via Giuseppe Gabetti, 20147
+39 02 8905 8306
maremilano.org

② Teatro alla Scala, Duomo
World-famous operatics

Considered by many to be the "temple of opera", the Teatro alla Scala (commonly known as La Scala) was built in 1776 while the city was under Austrian rule. Between composers, conductors and singers, many of the past and present's greatest have passed through its neoclassical arches, from Rossini and Verdi to Toscanini and Maria Callas.

With the season starting on 7 December each year (the day of the premiere as well as the feast day of the city's patron saint, Ambrose), the calendar ranges from opera and symphonic music to ballet. Getting your tickets well in advance is highly recommended but, should you not have any luck, sign up for a guided tour of the theatre's velvet stalls.
2 Via Filodrammatici, 20121
+39 02 88 791
teatroallascala.org

Oh I do rather like those pantaloons...

Let's dance

01 Plastic, Ripamonti:
Famous for its cheerful,
raucous atmosphere, this
club has been open since
1980 and over the years
has attracted visitors such
as Madonna, Keith Haring
and David Bowie.
15 Via Gargano, 20139

02 Fabrique, Linate: Huge
former warehouse where
up to 4,000 people can
dance to big-ticket
international DJs.
fabriquemilano.it

**03 Sala Venezia, Porta
Venezia:** A smartly
re-adapted *balera*, this
is a traditional ballroom
where youngsters
can tackle old-school
dances and truly do
their *nonna* proud.
+39 02 204 3765

③
LaVerdi, Navigli
Concerted effort

The Orchestra Sinfonica di Milano
Giuseppe Verdi was created in
1993 for young musicians and to
make classical music accessible to
everyone. In 1999 it found its home
in this wood-panelled auditorium,
once a 1920s silent cinema with a
beautiful façade.
　Chances are you'll be able to
listen to Beethoven's symphonies
for about €15 – and then there's
everything from chamber music to
jazz. Also keep an eye out for film
screenings such as *The Godfather*
or Fellini's *Amarcord*, with live
soundtracks from the orchestra.
Largo Gustav Mahler, 20136
+39 02 8338 9401
laverdi.org

Piccolo Teatro Strehler, Castello
Performance spaces

The Piccolo Teatro was founded in
1947 as "the theatre for all" and its
mission is still to stage a variety of
shows for the broadest audience.
There are three separate venues to
the Piccolo: the Teatro Grassi, the
Teatro Studio Melato (dedicated to
experimental shows) and the 968-
seat Teatro Strehler.
　The theatre's programme
ranges from Shakespeare, Chekhov
and avant garde productions to
dance, film screenings and debates,
so there's plenty even for non-
Italian speakers.
1 Largo Greppi, 20121
+39 02 4241 1889
piccoloteatro.org

⑤
Circolo Magnolia, Segrate
Woodland features

Milan is a big city with surprisingly
few venues for concerts but Circolo
Magnolia does its best to make up
for the musical paucity. Located
practically next door to Linate
airport, it's so far removed from
the city centre that it is completely
surrounded by woods, which means
that there's no one to complain
about the booming music from
the many outdoor performances.
　Across its four stages, the venue
hosts the annual Mi Ami festival
of Italian musicians and attracts
the kind of international acts that
would otherwise skip over Milan
between shows in Paris and Berlin.
Drink and ticket prices are always
affordable, which brings in young
people of all stripes.
*41 Via Circonvallazione
Idroscalo, 20090*
+39 02 756 1046
circolomagnolia.it

Cinemas
Moving pictures

Milan on film

01 Miracolo a Milano, 1951:
An optimistic 1950s
classic directed by Vittorio
de Sica that's imbued
with social critiques on
post-war inequality.
Orphan Totò receives
magic powers and uses
them to fight for the poor.

02 I Am Love, 2009: This
beautifully shot and
sensuous film by Luca
Guadagnino features Tilda
Swinton as the head of
a modern-day wealthy
Milanese family that
inhabits the Villa Necchi
Campiglio (see pages 93
and 111) – where much
of the film is set.

03 La Classe Operaia Va in
Paradiso, 1971:
Dedicated factory worker
Lulù undergoes a political
awakening after he loses
a finger while operating
one of the machines in this
scathing drama set in a
1970s suburban factory.

04 Rocco e i Suoi Fratelli,
1960: Like many southern
Italian families did in the
1960s, Rocco and his
family – the Parondi
– move to Milan in search
of work and a better life. A
showpiece by celebrated
director Luchino Visconti.

05 Via Montenapoleone,
1986: Its cinematic
qualities may be debatable
but this film by the king
of Italian lowbrow, Carlo
Vanzina, bears witness to
and perfectly encapsulates
the "Milano da Bere"
years: the 1980s era of
yuppies, opportunism and
ruthless social climbing.

①
Anteo Palazzo del Cinema,
Porta Garibaldi
Lights, camera, action

Milan's cinema offering has
been somewhat lacklustre in
recent years: the Corso Vittorio
Emanuele, once nicknamed the
"Broadway del Cinema", lost the
moniker long ago and few quality
screens remain. However, Anteo
Palazzo del Cinema hopes to turn
things around.

This new venue, which opened
in September 2017 following a
€5.2m overhaul, features nine
screens, a library, a cinema-
restaurant and a café operated
by Eataly. Visitors can also enjoy
outdoor screenings at the adjoining
courtyard of the Chiesa di Santa
Maria Incoronata. Unfortunately
for non-Italian speakers, most
films are dubbed. But even if the
picture's over your head, drop
in for a drink at the bar, which
is open until 01.00.
8 Piazza XXV Aprile, 20122
+39 02 4391 2769
spaziocinema.info

Language lessons

Italian cinema has long
favoured dubbing to subtitles
but you can often catch a
screening in its original
language at these three venues.

01 Milano Odeon, Duomo:
A monumental art deco
venue with 10 screens.
thespacecinema.it

02 Spazio Oberdan,
Porta Venezia:
A smaller cinema showing
classics, independents
and documentaries.
oberdan.cinetecamilano.it

03 Colosseo, Città Studi:
Near the university district,
this one is cheap, cheerful
and shows all the latest
blockbusters, with tickets
starting at €6.
ilregnodelcinema.com

Media round-up
Word on the street

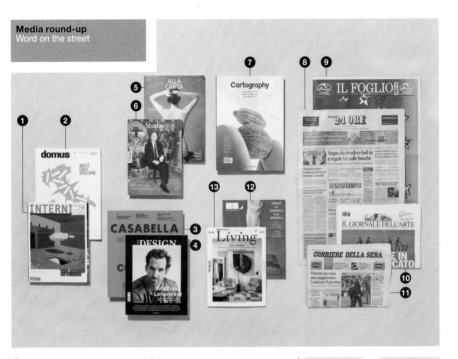

❶
Newspapers and magazines
Reading material

The publishing industry in Italy largely gravitates around Rome and Milan: the former may be the seat of most of the political big-hitters but the latter boasts the country's best business and design titles.

Magazines such as ❶ *Interni*, ❷ *Domus* and ❸ *Casabella* have been documenting and shaping the international interiors industry for decades. *Interni*, founded in 1954, is the youngest: it's now led by Gilda Bojardi, has 10 issues a year and a coveted annual design index. *Domus* and *Casabella* were both born in 1928 and have had illustrious names steering the ship: architects Gio Ponti and Guido Marangoni respectively. ❹ *Icon Design* first hit newsstands in 2015 and features interviews with the industry's big names alongside shoots stacked with covetable furniture.

A new wave of independent titles has also found fertile ground here. ❺ *Alla Carta* takes a sideways glance at fashion, art and design through the lens of food, while ❻ *Rivista Studio* is a quarterly spanning affairs and culture (plus excellent one-to-ones with interesting characters from Paolo Sorrentino to Massimo Bottura). With its large format and lush photography, ❼ *Cartography* looks like a travel magazine of yesteryear but was only founded in 2016.

Some of Italy's main dailies are also edited in Milan. ❽ *Il Sole 24 Ore* is where you'll find the authoritative financial news coverage. Smaller in circulation but not in format, ❾ *Il Foglio* presents centrist, conservative views, while ❿ *Il Giornale dell'Arte* has weighty opinions on all things cultural. Battling with Rome-based *La Repubblica* for prominence as the nation's biggest daily, the ⓫ *Corriere della Sera* is the city's go-to news source.

Finally, both *Il Sole 24 Ore* and *Corriere* have sleek monthlies: the former's ⓬ *Il* is a smart lifestyle read, while ⓭ *Living Corriere* is an interiors title that more than holds its own against its older cousins.

Kiosks

The *edicola* (newsagent) is an important fixture of Italian neighbourhood life and a social aggregator like no other. Residents gather here to purchase their daily dose of news but also to vivaciously discuss the latest political events (or simply to gossip).

Most gravitate to their local stand but it's worth making the trip to Fabrizio Prestinari's kiosk (*see page 135*) in Brera, which has won a following among journalists at the nearby *Corriere della Sera* offices. The tiny stall packs in the best (and most obscure) printed goods from around the world. Let Prestinari guide you through the jam-packed offering.
Largo Claudio Treves, 20121
+39 02 659 5290

Design and architecture
── Unexpected pleasures

Compared to Rome, Venice or Florence, Milan has historically drawn the short straw when it comes to urban architecture, with the words "grey" and "industrial" often bandied around. Today it's a different story: Milan is booming and many are proclaiming a "second miracle" (referring to the *miracolo economico* years of the 1950s and 1960s). And with a host of striking new cultural and commercial constructions, it's hard to disagree.

It's about time too, as the architectural and design history of Milan is unique. From the gothic spires of the Duomo to lashings of Liberty decoration and the crystalline precision of modernists such as Gio Ponti, Milan truly is a built treasure trove. There's a kaleidoscope of architectural movements, from the ancient (such as the 4th-century Basilica di Sant'Ambrogio) to the contemporary (such as the CityLife and Porta Nuova areas). Read on for some of the many rewards that await.

Contemporary
Magnificent modern

①
Fondazione Giangiacomo Feltrinelli, Porta Garibaldi
Urban renewal

Designed by Swiss architects Herzog & de Meuron and completed in 2016, this glass-and-stone structure houses a library named after publisher and leftwing activist Giangiacomo Feltrinelli, who died in murky circumstances in 1972. There are also reading spaces, offices and classrooms.

On a site scarred by wartime bombing, the five-floor building has transformed the area. It appears like a glass loaf of bread, which when sliced reveals a stereotypical pitched-roof house.
5 Viale Pasubio, 20154
+39 02 495 8341
fondazionefeltrinelli.it

2

Fondazione Prada, Ripamonti
Going for gold

Fondazione Prada is one of the city's premier arts-and-culture venues (*see page 94*) but many visitors come for the architecture alone. Rem Koolhaas' Rotterdam-based OMA practice reimagined seven existing buildings of a former distillery and added three new structures to them: a gallery, cinema and tower. "Old and new, horizontal and vertical, wide and narrow, white and black, open and enclosed" is how Koolhaas describes the project, emphasising the Fondazione's contradictions.

There's also a café designed by Wes Anderson (*see page 37*), a standalone cinema building covered in mirrors and the so-called "haunted house" (dating from 1910), the exterior of which is painted in dazzling 24-carat gold leaf for all-out bling.
2 Largo Isarco, 20139
+ 39 02 5666 2611
fondazioneprada.org

③

Bosco Verticale, Isola
High-rise greenery

These two towers – along with the neighbouring UniCredit – form the centrepiece of the Porta Nuova area to the north of the city. The creation of architects Studio Boeri, this "Vertical Forest", which was completed in 2014, is a clear response to the issues of environmental responsibility in an urban development. Planted with 900 trees, bushes and other flora, each tower is equivalent to 20,000 sq m of forest and offers a striking and ever-changing façade.

Botanical experts were employed to carefully choose and cultivate greenery that could handle the varying altitudes and direction of the exterior; the foliage produces humidity, absorbs CO_2 and dust particles and releases oxygen. It's a surreal sight but one that has won the approval of local birds, butterflies and bees as well as the jury of the International Highrise Award in 2014.
Via Gaetano de Castillia, 20124

Well isn't this
coming up roses

Expo Milano 2015

Back in 2015, the city of Milan was filled with consternation at the prospect of hosting the World's Fair. It wasn't the first time it had done so – the city held the event in 1906 – but with the country barely out of economic crisis, allegations of corrupt contractors flowing thick and fast, and a price tag reaching a staggering €13bn, including the cost of upgrading transport links, concern was high and the project seemed doomed to fail. Nonetheless, the gates opened and by the end of the year some 22 million visitors had flooded in.

The Milanese and guests from around the world were wowed by more than 70 pavilions set over 110 hectares. A special Expo Passport was introduced encouraging visitors to collect stamps at each country's exhibition. Milan was widely seen to do what it does best: put on a show. A spike in tourism led to notable growth in the economy according to experts. Perhaps more than that, Expo's legacy is a regained sense of civic confidence. More tangibly, the Expo site will be transformed into a 35,000 sq m centre for biomedical research and development.

Tall order
───
In a city increasingly in love with skyscrapers, the UniCredit Tower, completed in 2011, is currently Italy's tallest. Housing the HQ of the country's biggest bank, César Pelli's design features a tapering spire that has redefined Milan's skyline.
unicreditgroup.eu

❹
Tre Torri, CityLife
Triple whammy

This huge, almost perfectly square-shaped piece of land, clearly visible on the street plan of Milan, was until 2005 the site of the Fiera Milano exhibition hall prior to it relocating to its new home in suburban Rho. A consortium of world-famous architects – Daniel Libeskind, Zaha Hadid and Arata Isozaki – won a tender to develop the 360,000 sq m that would become the CityLife neighbourhood, the centrepiece of which is Tre Torri (Three Towers). Each was responsible for designing a striking edifice.

First to be completed was Torre Isozaki whose slender rectangular structure (210 metres in height) is graced with the gentle bulges of glass-curtain-like façades. Insurers Allianz are the first occupants of the building and, not to be outdone, rival Italian company Generali will move into Hadid's twisting, sinuous and slightly shorter (170 metres) effort. Libeskind's curved tower, which has been likened to a metal banana, is set to be finished in about 2020.
Piazza Tre Torri, 20145
+ 39 02 862 041
city-life.it

⑤
Università Bocconi, Bocconi
Cool for school

This prestigious university has long aimed to ensure that its facilities match its academic output. The drive for architectural excellence began with Giuseppe Pagano, who designed the main building in 1937, kickstarting a modernist campus par excellence.

A 2002 competition resulted in Dublin-based Grafton Architects bestowing monumental new lecture theatres and classrooms. The Aula Magna (Great Hall) seems to defy gravity and is best appreciated at the corner of Viale Bligny and Via Guglielmo Röntgen.
25 Via Roberto Sarfatti, 20100
+ 39 02 5836 3434
unibocconi.it

❻
Santa Maria Annunciata, Chiesa Rossa
See the light

In 1996, the priest at this outer-city church invited US minimalist artist Dan Flavin to create an installation that would form part of the restoration and renewal of the 1932 structure designed by architect Giovanni Muzio.

Flavin, an Irish Catholic who was brought up in New York and had studied to join the priesthood, created "Untitled" using green, blue, pink, golden and ultraviolet light to illuminate the church's ceiling, columns and walls. The mesmerising work was completed two days before Flavin's death.
24 Via Neera, 20141
parrocchiachiesarossa.net

Three influential architects of the 20th century

01 Giovanni Muzio (1893-1982): Starting out in the early 1920s, Muzio was considered something of a radical with his novecento style. His Ca' Brütta (Ugly Building) (*see page 112*) in particular was a break with the past due to its simple, curved exterior. He also drew on historical references and a grander style can be seen in the Palazzo dell'Arengario (*see page 113*) and Palazzo dell'Arte, now the Triennale di Milano (*see page 92*).

02 Gio Ponti (1891-1979): Ponti's prolific career has probably done more than any other to shape modern Milan. Graduating from the prestigious Politecnico di Milano, he collaborated on low-key projects (including with Giovanni Muzio) before the boom years of the 1950s saw him dazzle. He worked on more than 60 buildings across the city although his most celebrated success is the Pirelli Tower.

03 Piero Portaluppi (1888-1967): Renowned for his luxurious yet restrained neoclassical style, Portaluppi changed the face of Milan from the 1920s to the 1960s. He started his career in the industrial sector designing power plants, before going on to imagine residential works for the Milanese bourgeoisie. His vast body of work includes Planetario Hoepli, Villa Necchi Campiglio (*see page 111*) and Casa Crespi.

1950s and 1960s boom
Growth spurt

1

Susa Auto Silo, Risorgimento
Multistorey magic

Off the beaten track it may be but a visit to this *silo* (car park) is well worth it and is proof of Milan's technological prowess in the postwar period. Completed in 1968 by Carlo Perogalli, it was the largest facility of its kind in Europe and even today you'll find little like it outside Manhattan or Tokyo.

Over 22 levels, 500 cast-concrete cells were created to allow cars to be hydraulically lifted and slotted into place. A full-height wall of glass with a viewing ramp lets you watch the whole process.
5 Via Gaspare Gozzi, 20129
+ 39 02 738 3443
susaautosilo.com

2
Pirelli Tower, Centrale
Perfect form

Built between 1956 and 1958 by architecture-and-engineering duo Gio Ponti and Pier Luigi Nervi for tyre-maker Pirelli, this building is the embodiment of Milan's "economic miracle". When topped with its distinctive sheet roof, which appears to levitate above the rest of the structure, its 127-metre height made it the tallest office building in Europe.

The proportions of the building are intriguing, being surprisingly long (76 metres) and thin (only 21 metres wide), with a tapering floorplan adding extra sleekness. The tower is currently the seat of Lombardy's Regional Assembly.
22 Via Fabio Filzi, 20124

③

Torre Velasca, Guastalla
Room up top

From street level this tower, built between 1951 and 1958 by Milan architects BBPR and Ernesto Nathan Rogers (cousin of Richard Rogers), is both brooding and slightly menacing: are we in Milan or Gotham City?

The distinctive top-heavy shape comes from the increased floorplan of the 20th to 24th floors, which were designed to house "villas in the sky", and resembles that of medieval watchtowers. The perfect abode for a certain winged superhero perhaps?
3-5 Piazza Velasca, 20122

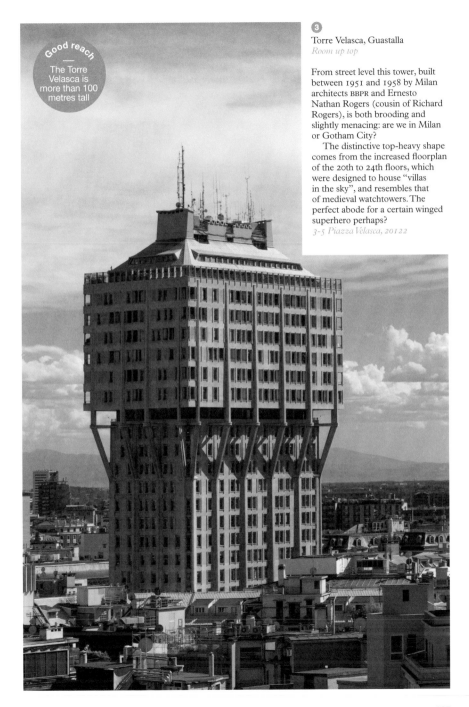

Good reach
—
The Torre Velasca is more than 100 metres tall

④

13 Corso Italia, Missori
Ship shape

The plot of land on which this mixed-use complex stands was bombed extensively during the Second World War and subsequent development of the site (from 1949 to 1957) filled it with a dynamic structure. Roman architect Luigi Moretti used radical plans to bring drama and even a sense of vertigo with the creation of a tapered seven-storey office and apartment building, which he placed perpendicular to the pavement.

The striking effect earned the building the nickname "La Vela" due to its sail-like shape, which stretches out above the street below like a modernist tallship.
13 Corso Italia, 20122

⑤

Chiesa di San Francesco d'Assisi al Fopponino, La Maddalena
Divine intervention

As part of the archdiocese of Milan's plan to build 22 new churches to meet demographic expansion, and as a way in which to celebrate the Second Vatican Council, Gio Ponti was commissioned to design this church and accompanying parish buildings. The result, completed in 1964, is modern religious architecture at its best.

Ponti's search for perfect forms often brought him back to the crystal and here he uses the hexagon as a motif inside and out, while the façade is covered in small, grey ceramic tiles.
41 Via Paolo Giovio, 20144

Oscar worthy
───
Giorgio Mondadori, chairman of publishers Mondadori, was so in awe of the Palácio Itamaraty (Foreign Ministry) in Brasília that he asked its creator, Oscar Niemeyer, to build him a new HQ in Milan. The result, completed in 1975 at Segrate, is one of the architect's greatest works.

Postwar residential
Building blocks

❶

Monte Amiata Housing
Development, Gallaratese
Experimental homes

Built between 1967 and 1974, to
an urban design co-ordinated by
Carlo Aymonino and involvement
from postmodernist poster-boy
Aldo Rossi, this terracotta-coloured
complex is a must-see for anyone
with an interest in social-housing
architecture. The layout comprises
five blocks of varying forms and
sizes that have been designed as a
whole; three geometric shapes –
cube, parallelepiped (slanted cube)
and cylinder – and primary-colour
accents act as overarching motifs.

In true brutalist fashion,
the architects ignored all links
to context and instead chose to
revive historic concepts of the
city: the street, the square, the
shared balcony and, perhaps
most pleasingly, the theatre: the
amphitheatre at the heart of
the complex is a true urban gem.
47 Via Enrico Falck, 20151

*Oh I do
like a pop
of colour*

Ettore Sottsass

Given that much of Milan's 20th-century architecture led in some way to the creation of postmodernism, it seems only natural that the city should also produce Ettore Sottsass, one of the most important postmodernist designers that was.

Starting work for Adriano Olivetti in 1956, by 1970 Sottsass had designed the Valentine typewriter, which thanks to its pleasing shape and bright colour became a must-have design accessory rather than a standard piece of office equipment. In 1981 he set up design consultancy Sottsass Associati, which garnered a slew of Italian and international clients.

His definitive moment came the same year when he founded Memphis (*see page 50*), a collective of furniture designers and artists who, over a few years, set the tone of the postmodernist movement. With their improbable angles, bright colours and eccentric shapes, pieces such as the Carlton bookcase, Beverly sideboard and Tahiti lamp became must-haves for the wealthy sets of Milan, Manhattan and beyond. With its reserved etiquette and design know-how, Milan is still very much influenced by Sottsass today.

And here you have the Colonne di San Lorenzo...

②
Torre al Parco, Magenta
Right side of the tracks

From afar this residential tower block might appear unremarkable but close up its elegantly modern traits are revealed. Architects Vico Magistretti and Franco Longoni used only 400 sq m of the 1,200 sq m available so as to maintain plenty of greenery and not impact on views to the Parco Sempione across the railway tracks.

Built between 1953 and 1956, the 20-storey tower has an L-shaped plan, with just four apartments occupying each floor. The simple façades are surprisingly vibrant, in part thanks to the uniform red blinds that were also specified in the plans.
2-4 Via Revere, 20123

③
Via Dezza Apartments, Tortona
The place for Ponti

Built by Gio Ponti in collaboration with Antonio Fornaroli and Alberto Rosselli, and completed in 1957, this is where Ponti worked for some time and lived at the end of his life. His abode on the eighth floor and the rest of the block show off the principles of the *casa all'Italiana* (Italian home) that he devised to great effect.

Ponti's flair for the decorative means that ceramic floors are festooned with colourful diagonal stripes. The architect's former office is home to the Gio Ponti Archives (*see page 97*) and can be visited by appointment.
49 Via Giuseppe Dezza, 20144
gioponti.org

Rationalist modernist
Form and function

Centre stage
——
Popular venue
for fashion
and design
events

①
Casa Rustici, Sempione
Clean living

This 1935 apartment building, a
collaboration between Giuseppe
Terragni and Pietro Lingeri, is a
beacon of rationalist architecture.
Terragni was keen to contrast the
drab urban blocks that surround
the site – as he was to do with
the Casa del Fascio in Como (*see
page 121*) – so two structures were
created and connected by a series
of bridges and flying balconies.

On the sixth floor the blocks are
unified further by way of a covered
bridge crossing the space between
the buildings to create one large
penthouse apartment.
36 Corso Sempione, 20154

②
Villa Necchi Campiglio, Monforte
Ahead of its time

Built for the prominent industrialist
Necchi Campiglio family by
Piero Portaluppi, this mansion
epitomises the Milanese style and
sophistication of the 1930s. The
family wanted a refined home with
every mod con of the time, so the
architect dutifully kitted it out with
elevators, intercoms and Milan's
first private heated swimming pool.

Great attention was given to
materials, nowhere more so than
in the exquisite veranda that serves
as an internal winter garden. The
house was immortalised in Luca
Guadagnino's 2009 film *I Am Love*.
14 Via Mozart, 20122
+39 02 7634 0121
visitfai.it/villanecchi

③
Ca' Brütta, Porta Nuova
Ugly truth

Today, this curved building on
the corner of Via della Moscova
and Piazza Stati Uniti d'America
may not seem revolutionary but
when construction began in 1919 it
represented a radical break with the
past. It's now regarded as the first
modernist building in Milan.

Architect Giovanni Muzio
adopted a methodical approach
to stripping back the classical
style of the day. His sober façade,
with alcoves and muted details,
inspired the novecento style seen
throughout the city. Although
labelled "brütta" (ugly), there's
something beautiful about it.
14 Via della Moscova, 20121
cabrutta.it

④
Palazzo Fidia, Porta Venezia
Brilliant brick

Occupying a triangular corner
site, this eight-storey apartment
building is the most intriguing work
of lesser-known architect Aldo
Andreani. Although fundamentally
rationalist, Palazzo Fidia is
imbued with several of Andreani's
individualistic quirks.

Using typical Lombard
materials (most notably brick),
he employs many creative tricks to
decorate the façade: arches, niches,
dwarf balustrades, bay windows
(unusual for Italy) and pediments
are apparent throughout. To top
it off, exaggerated eaves point to
Chicago and Frank Lloyd Wright
rather than bourgeois Milan.
2 Via Luigi Amedeo Melegari, 20122

⑤
Palazzo dell'Arengario, Duomo
Rooted in history

The twin gatehouse-like buildings
on the south side of the Piazza del
Duomo are the result of attempts
to give the city centre an imposing
feel during the 1930s Fascist era
(Mussolini gave public speeches
from here). A host of prominent
architects were involved in the
project, including Piero Portaluppi
and Giovanni Muzio – whose
stylistic traits are apparent in the
symmetrical façades.

One of the buildings was turned
into the Museo del Novecento
(*see page 91*) in 2010 and hosts a
collection of modern artwork.
1 Via Marconi, 20122
+ 39 02 8844 4061
museodelnovecento.org

Liberty style
Decorative designs

❶
Casa Galimberti, Porta Venezia
Sumptuous façades

Casa Galimberti is an ode to the
flamboyant frivolity that is Italian
Liberty. The exteriors of this corner
building are covered with vivid
painted ceramic tiles depicting
nubile figures and floral displays,
all set on a gilded backdrop.

It was completed in 1905 for
the Galimberti brothers, who
wanted to take advantage of the
new electric tramway nearby
by investing in an opulent
development. Architect Giovanni
Battista Bossi duly delivered and
the building now stands in Milan's
Liberty cluster, with the less-
colourful Casa Guazzoni (also
by Bossi) further along the street.
3 Via Marcello Malpighi, 20129

Design fairs

The annual Salone del Mobile
(*see page 79*) is the world's
largest trade fair specialising in
furniture, lighting and product
design. It was first held in 1961
and only showcased Italian
objects but has grown (and
grown) far beyond that; so
much so that in 2005 the Fiera
Milano complex moved to its
vast new home in Rho on the
outskirts of the city.

Today the accompanying
Fuorisalone (Fringe Salone)
includes some 1,500 events
and exhibitions spread across
the city.

Palazzo Berri-Meregalli,
Porta Venezia
Dark star

This imposing residential building, built for the Berri-Meregalli family in 1913 by Giulio Ulisse Arata, is perhaps one of the last exponents of the Liberty style. Although laden with symbolic decoration, it also has strong historical references (such as the Romanesque-inspired main tower), a departure that was widely criticised at the time.

There's plenty to look at: up high, the clinging sculpted muscular figures; and at street level, the ironwork of master blacksmith Alessandro Mazzucotelli. Arata's creation has a gloomy sense of foreboding but it's a ghoulish treat.
8 Via Cappuccini, 20122

①

Palazzo Castiglioni, Porta Venezia
Bottoms up

Keen to flaunt his wealth, engineer and industrialist Ermenegildo Castiglioni commissioned architect Giuseppe Sommaruga to build him a mansion. Money was not the only thing on show; he also wanted to demonstrate something avant garde. Sommaruga followed the Liberty style prominent at the time and this grand palazzo was built between 1901 and 1904.

The façade's contrast between smooth and decorated surfaces has dramatic impact. But not as much as the two nudes at the entrance. Earning the name "House of the Buttocks", they caused such offence that they were removed.
47 Corso Venezia, 20121

①
Galleria Vittorio Emanuele II,
Duomo
Shopping showcase

No building in Italy epitomises the national flair for retail commerce more than this shopping arcade, built between 1865 and 1877 and dedicated to the king of the newly unified country. Connecting the Duomo and La Scala, this is the prototype bourgeois shopping-mall experience – and for high glamour and opulence, the original has never been surpassed.

The Galleria stands apart from similar arcades in Brussels, London and St Petersburg due to its monumental scale and engineering audacity, especially evident in the huge dome. This was largely the work of French contractors and the glass came from the famous Saint-Gobain factory. For good luck – and that (slightly corny) Milanese experience – stare up while twisting your heel on a mosaic bull's private parts.
Piazza del Duomo, 20121
ingalleria.com

Designs on study
————

Head to the Triennale di
Milano's basement library to
top up your Milanese design
know-how. It's free; just sign
in to make use of the design
and architecture books and
magazines and settle down
in suitably studious
surroundings.
triennale.org

Lifting the lid
The arcade
is topped with
an iron-and-
glass roof

❷

Albergo Diurno Venezia,
Porta Venezia
Art deco bathing

Albergo Diurno Venezia opened
in 1925 as a one-stop location for
bathing facilities, thermal spas,
barbers' shops, manicures and
even a travel agent. With the main
railway station then situated at the
nearby Piazza della Repubblica
and new apartments springing
up (usually without baths) there
was a market for this kind of daily
indulgence.

With the station relocating
and the arrival of improved
domestic plumbing, the bathhouse
closed. What is left is a snapshot
of 1920s Milan. Openings to this
underground art deco treasure
are sporadic but usually coincide
with Salone del Mobile and Open
House events.
Piazza Guglielmo Oberdan, 20124
fondoambiente.it

③
Cimitero Monumentale,
Monumentale
Grave matters

Like a city within a city, Milan's
largest cemetery was laid out to the
plans of architect Carlo Maciachini
in 1866. Once through the huge
neo-Romanesque entrance, which
also acts as the *famedio* (hall of
fame), a network of streets, avenues
and squares lies within.

An *edicola* (family tomb) might
indulge in grand folly in order to
show off wealth. With designs by
the likes of Giannino Castiglioni,
Gio Ponti and Piero Portaluppi, it's
an outdoor museum as much as a
final resting place.
Piazzale Cimitero Monumentale,
20154
comune.milano.it

④
Stazione Centrale, Centrale
End of the line

Milan's Stazione Centrale is easily
one of the world's most impressive
stations, as well as being one of
Europe's largest. Works started to
replace the small, quaint French-
style affair down the road in 1906
(it's now fully demolished) but it
wasn't until Ulisse Stacchini won a
design competition in 1912 that the
railway station began to take on
its current bombastic character.

Progress was slow, resulting
in the building featuring several
architectural styles. The main
feature, however, is the sheer
generosity of space; three vast
vaulted galleries (for carriages,
tickets and waiting) have to be
traversed before reaching your
train on one of the 24 tracks. Add
to this the eclectic details outside
(winged horses) and motifs from
the Fascist era on the interior and
you get a jaw-dropping building
that is a worthy destination in itself.
1 Piazza Duca d'Aosta, 20125
milanocentrale.it

①
Castello Sforzesco, Castello
Tower of strength

This vast castle was commissioned
by Francesco Sforza in 1450 to
be built on top of the fortress
constructed by the Visconti
(the preceding lords of Milan).
Renaissance sculptor and architect
Antonio di Pietro Averlino, known
as Filarete, designed the huge
central tower true to the Sforza
family's wish to dominate the city.

It was to become one of the
largest citadels in Europe and
allowed early French, Spanish and
then Napoleonic rulers to control
the Milanese. Today the castle
houses nine museums.
Piazza Castello, 20121
+39 02 8846 3700
milanocastello.it

①

Trams
On the right track

As in Lisbon or San Francisco, the rumbling tram is part of Milan's urban identity. With 17 lines and 182km of track, however, the Italian city has far more trams than its Portuguese and Californian cousins.

The most iconic car is the ATM Class 1500 Series, which was designed in 1928 using the Cleveland-made Peter Witt streetcar as a model. Even today many of these are lovingly maintained and retain original wooden interiors. You'll find a bunch of them at the depot on Via Messina.

③

Basilica di Sant'Ambrogio, Sant'Ambrogio
Back in time

For an experience of the ancient, spiritual foundations of the city, a visit to this basilica is a must. It's possibly Milan's oldest surviving church, built by the city's patron saint, Saint Ambrose, between 379AD and 386AD and remains architecturally unaltered.

Unusually it has both a Canon's Tower and a Monk's Tower, showing the rivalry between the church and monastery that share it. Inside, be sure to glance up at the golden ceiling of the Sacello di San Vittore in Ciel d'Oro.
15 Piazza Sant'Ambrogio, 20123
basilicasantambrogio.it

②

Case di ringhiera
Home sweet homes

Originating from the early 1900s, the *case di ringhiera* (railing houses) are traditional Milanese dwellings. Now highly sought after, it wasn't always so; these were tenement houses built for poor workers with minimal sanitation facilities (a whole building might share a single toilet). These days the small apartments, which have long balconies set around pretty courtyards, define Milanese gentrification, especially in the Navigli and Brera districts.

②

Duomo di Milano, Duomo
The big one

Construction began on Milan's most famous landmark – and one of the largest church buildings in the world – at the behest of Gian Galeazzo Visconti, lord of Milan, in 1386. But it wasn't for another six centuries that the final details and missing spires were completed.

The Duomo is a gothic celebration, with its forest of stalagmite-like spires, rows of flying buttresses and gargoyles aplenty. A trip to the roof is a timeless experience. Look up to the golden "Madonnina", which until the 1960s was the city's highest point.
Piazza del Duomo, 20122
+ 39 02 7202 3375
duomomilano.it

④
Courtyards
Inner sanctums

Like the city itself, Milan's courtyards convey discrete elegance and ostentation, available only to those who are able to appreciate it (or seek it out). The old maxim about not judging a book by its cover certainly rings true when walking the city's often unassuming streets.

Whether it's the ornate public grandeur of Palazzo Marino (city hall) and Palazzo di Brera, or the countless smaller private palazzos (such as those of the Borromeo d'Adda and Belgioioso families) that on occasion allow their inner tranquillity to be revealed, Milan's courtyards are windows into the soul of the place.

❸
Rooftop gardens
View from above

Many of Milan's rooftop spaces are home to pocket-sized floral oases, offering residents secluded spots in which to have breakfast or entertain guests. In the warmer months these grow so abundantly that you can catch tantalising glimpses of them from the streets below. Although the best are private, befriend a local and they might just invite you for a coffee among the fig trees.

⑤

Enzo Mari bollards
Concrete treat

Italy has a long history of entrusting even the most banal street furniture to the hands of designers. In the 1980s Milan commissioned famed artist and designer Enzo Mari to create a traffic bollard. The resulting concrete "panettones", as they were dubbed, were a success and, decades on, hundreds of them can still be spotted around the city.

⑥

Metro signage
Way to go

Influential Dutch-born graphic designer Bob Noorda started work on the signage for Milan Metro's Line 1 in 1962. (Noorda was to go on to work with New York subway scheme designer Massimo Vignelli in the 1970s). Although it might come as standard now, Noorda's Metro scheme was the first to use indicator strips with a clear band of colour that repeated the station name at the level where passengers could read it from inside the train.

He was also first to ensure that the same colour (red, in this case) was used on all surrounding architectural elements.

⑦

Shop and bar signs
Light it up

From pharmacies and hardware stores to toy shops and trattorias, Milanese business-owners have long had a tendency to vie for customers by way of old-fashioned shop signs. Either in the light-box variety, spelled out with shaped Perspex lettering or painted in blocky typefaces, family names and company titles are emblazoned across the city's façades.

When it comes to selling alcohol, however, neon is king. Milan is home to many distilleries and brands – such as Campari and Aperol – so the visual marketing of booze comes naturally. Bar Basso (*see page 47*) is a great place to observe this mix of signage.

Lake escapes
—— Head for the water

Milan's proximity to some of northern Italy's most spectacular natural scenery means that the city is often used as a springboard for reaching other places.

Lakes Maggiore, Como and Iseo are all within striking distance and have long been the weekend getaway of choice for the Milanese. Their pristine shores are dotted with ornate villas, welcoming hotels and quaint towns ripe for exploring.

Here's our pick of the cultural sites, architectural gems and blissful boltholes worth getting out of town for. Dive right in.

01

02

03

04

05

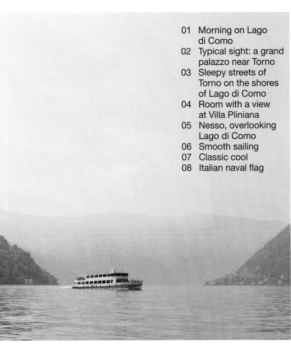

01 Morning on Lago di Como
02 Typical sight: a grand palazzo near Torno
03 Sleepy streets of Torno on the shores of Lago di Como
04 Room with a view at Villa Pliniana
05 Nesso, overlooking Lago di Como
06 Smooth sailing
07 Classic cool
08 Italian naval flag

Address book

Como Classic Boats, Lago di Como
Cruise the lake on an old-school Tritone 81 or opt for a private tour and kick back.
comoclassicboats.com

Lido di Segrino, near Lago di Como
Swim in the emerald waters of Lago del Segrino from this contemporary bathing complex designed by Marco Castelletti.
+39 031 547 7692

A Gi Emme, near Lago di Como
Owner Adriano Monti stocks well-chosen men's and womenswear brands, including Zanone, Salvatore Piccolo and Massimo Alba.
agiemme.com

Casa del Fascio, near Lago di Como
Architect Giuseppe Terragni's 1936 structure was commissioned as a municipal building during Mussolini's regime but today it stands as a modern masterpiece.
Piazza del Popolo, 22100

Villa d'Este, Lago di Como
The 16th-century renaissance residence of the Este princes and a hotel since 1873.
villadeste.com

06

07   08

01

02 03

04

05 06

07

Address book

**Il Sereno Hotel,
Lago di Como**
Watch the boats sail by
from the lake-view suites
at this Patricia Urquiola-
designed luxury hotel.
serenohotels.com

**Taverna Antico Agnello,
near Lago Maggiore**
A homely restaurant in the
stately 16th-century Villa Nigra.
Pair the hearty Piedmontese
dishes with a bottle of barolo.
ristoranteanticoagnello.com

**Isola Bella and Isola Madre,
Lago Maggiore**
Two islets belonging to the
noble Borromeo family, famed
for their lush gardens and
baroque architecture.
isoleborromee.it

**Il Maggiore Centro
Eventi Multifunzionale,
Lago Maggiore**
Dance, music and theatre
in a structure designed
by Madrileño architect
Salvador Pérez Arroyo.
ilmaggioreverbania.it

**Berlucchi vineyard,
near Lago d'Iseo**
Since 1955 the Berlucchi
family has been producing
arguably the region's finest
sparkling wine.
berlucchi.it

08 09

10

11 12

01–03 Il Sereno Hotel
04 Lido di Segrino
05 Isola Bella
06 Verdant balconies
on the shores of
Lago Maggiore
07 Villa d'Este
08–09 Berlucchi vineyard
10 Il Maggiore Centro
Eventi Multifunzionale
11 Casa del Fascio
12 Mario Botta's Centro
Pastorale Papa
Giovanni XXIII near
Lago d'Iseo

Sport and fitness
—— On the move

The Milanese are a relatively active bunch. Chances are you'll encounter residents running through the city's leafy parks in the early hours, rowing along the glistening *navigli* on the weekend or, post-work, breaking a sweat in a fully equipped gym. The past few years have seen numerous bland chains sprout up across Milan but that's not to say that there's a shortage of independent options.

And remember: come rain or shine, many residents bid the city farewell at the weekend, whether to ski in the nearby mountains in the colder months or to decompress on the shores of a neighbouring lake (*see page 120*).

Here's a run-through of the best places for a spot of *esercizio fisico* – and, of course, a handful of tranquil spots for some well-deserved pampering.

Swimming pools
Making a splash

①

Ceresio 7, Sarpi
Alfresco lengths

Part of Dean and Dan Caten's mini empire (*see page 46*), this rooftop pool with chic cabanas and stunning skyline views attracts a ritzy crowd. Numbers are limited and booking in advance is recommended between June and September. A fixed €110 entrance allows access for a day and includes a towel and a rather fetching pair of sandals.

If you tire of reclining poolside there's also a hi-tech gym that runs classes from boxing to barre, plus a spa offering an array of treatments.
7 Via Ceresio, 20154
+39 02 3103 9221
ceresio7.com; ceresio7gym-spa.com

You can even exercise while sightseeing!

②

Piscina Cozzi, Porta Nuova
Swimming in style

Designed in 1934 by architect Luigi Secchi – the man behind the reconstruction of La Scala opera house after it was bombed in the Second World War – the Piscina Cozzi was restored to its former glory in 2004.

The complex is popular for its central location (a stone's throw from Piazza della Repubblica), proportions (the main pool is 33 metres long and five metres deep, making it an excellent choice for diving practice) and imposing architecture. Brush up on your technique with its programme of instructor-led courses.
35 Viale Tunisia, 20124
+39 02 659 9703

Strokes ahead
—
This was one of the city's first swimming facilities

③
Bagni Misteriosi, Porta Romana
Synchronised swimming

After years of abandonment, the Pier Lombardo Fondazione (the organisation behind the nearby Franco Parenti theatre) decided to revive this 1930s gem. Another masterpiece by rationalist architect Luigi Secchi (*see opposite*), today Bagni Misteriosi features two beautifully restored public pools and wide terraces popular with locals looking to catch some rays.

In summer, fees range according to the time of day; on Thursdays, the pools are open until midnight.
18 Via Carlo Botta, 20135
+ 39 02 8973 1800
bagnimisteriosi.com

Out and about
Hit the ground running

1
Arena Civica Gianni Brera,
Sempione
Best foot forward

Grab your running shoes and enjoy
a few laps around this 19th-century
stadium, which hosts sporting
events and concerts alike. The 400-
metre, eight-lane track is open to
the public year round and includes
high jump, long jump and javelin
platforms. Plus if you're into team
sports, there are areas for football,
basketball and rugby.

Patti Smith and Sting have
held concerts here and, with some
30,000 seats for spectators, runners
feel like they're in the limelight too.
2 Viale Giorgio Byron, 20154

*Why thank you,
I do have a
fine technique*

Autodromo Nazionale Monza

The Autodromo Nazionale
Monza has hosted the Italian
Grand Prix leg of the Formula 1
calendar since 1950 – it's one
of about 20 races held during
the annual championship – and
as one of the oldest tracks, to
many it's a bastion of the F1
sporting tradition.

The main race is on Sunday,
with qualifiers on the Friday
and Saturday before. Drivers
must complete 53 laps of the
5.8km circuit, equating to about
306km. The shoe-shaped
track requires both speed and
control; with demanding turns
such as the 180-degree Curva
Parabolica, it can test the most
seasoned driver.

Unlike the Monte Carlo
Grand Prix, where high hotel
prices and VIP guest lists make
the race inaccessible to most
fans, Monza is democratic.
Since it's only 15km from
Milan, many spectators stay in
the city. Tickets for qualifying
day start at about €50,
while centre-stage seats on
Sunday can fetch up to €750.
The buzzy atmosphere and
charming countryside make
for a thrilling day out.
formula1.com

②
Sport Master, Bullona
Having a ball

If the sunny weather makes you
want to hit a ball around, head to
Sport Master. Open seven days a
week from September to July, this
sports centre features six covered
tennis courts: four synthetic turf
and two hard courts.

Fees vary according to the time
of day and season but a one-hour
booking ranges between €25 and
€35, while for €50 you can improve
your skills with a one-on-one
45-minute lesson.
67 Via Govone, 20155
+ 39 02 349 4041
sportmaster.it

Grooming
Making the cut

① Antica Barbieria Colla, Duomo
Tried and tested

Always impeccably turned out, the staff at Antica Barbieria Colla are guardians of traditional men's grooming. Owner Franco Bompieri – who has seven decades of experience up his sleeves – is on hand to offer pearls of wisdom. Among his time-old techniques (the barbershop opened in 1904) is the use of a candle to singe split ends. For wet shaves, he lathers up a brush of subtly scented almond soap.

The shop sells its own line of lotions, balms and tonics, including a chamomile shampoo for blondes.
3 Via Gerolamo Morone, 20121
+39 02 874 312
anticabarbieriacolla.it

② Barberino's, Magenta
Take your time

Barberino's – whose pistachio-green interiors feature old-fashioned Sicilian barber chairs staffed by white-liveried *barbieri* – was founded by two bankers who wanted to revive the tradition of the neighbourhood barber.

Clients can choose from a trio of wet shaves: those with time to spare should opt for the hour-long Magenta treatment, featuring hot and cold towels plus an invigorating facial massage. Patrons can also try the brand's own line of grooming products, including a plant-based anti-ageing cream.
10 Corso Magenta, 20123
+39 02 8343 9447
barberinosworld.com

③ Tonsor Club, Brera
Cut above

If you find yourself lured into the heart of Brera by the smooth sound of jazz, there's a good chance that it's coming from Tonsor Club on Via Palermo.

Owners Stefano Coli and Mauro Bellini – creators of stellar Milanese salon Les Garçons de la rue – have created a smart, contemporary space featuring wooden furniture, exposed brickwork and white tiles which is as welcoming as it is relaxing. The top-notch service includes cuts, washes and hot-towel shaves.
15 Via Palermo, 20121
+39 02 495 33040
tonsorclub.com

Spas
Sit back and relax

Water feature

Jacuzzis can be found in the garden

1
QC Termemilano, Porta Romana
Do as the Romans did

Inspired by the philosophy of ancient baths, this hidden oasis in the city centre is housed in an 1800s building, originally a depot for horse-drawn trams.

Book an indoor session to enjoy the various saunas and steam baths, not forgetting the salt room, hydromassage and waterfall to fully relax your muscles. Or head outdoors, where Roman ruins surround groundwater whirlpools heated to 37c and the world's only tram converted into a sauna. Reserve a daytime slot or visit during the evening to relax under the stars.
2 Piazzale Medaglie d'Oro, 20135
+39 02 5519 9367
qcterme.com

Breathe easy
———
Tucked away in the inner courtyard of a former fashion atelier, City Zen is one of the city's top yoga destinations. Classes vary from meditative to flow and take place in a beautiful, green open space. Choose between group and solo sessions.
cityzen.it

2
Armani Spa, Quadrilatero della Moda
Lathered in luxury

With a breathtaking view over Milan's skyline from the Duomo to the futuristic skyscrapers of Porta Nuova, this spa on Armani Hotel's top floor is worth the visit for the vista alone. Try the sauna, steam bath and ice cascade then take a dip in the pool.

Armani Casa is responsible for the minimal design, as well as the oils and creams used in the anti-oxidant treatments. Custom massages, including the Jet-lag recovery, and half and full-day spa experiences are also available.
31 Via Alessandro Manzoni, 20121
+39 02 8883 8888
armanihotelmilano.com/en/spa

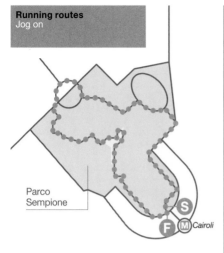

Parco
Sempione

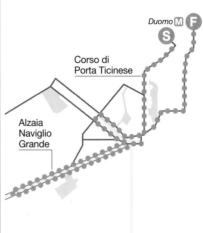

Duomo Ⓜ **F**
Ⓢ

Corso di
Porta Ticinese

Alzaia
Naviglio
Grande

Ⓢ
F Ⓜ *Cairoli*

 Parco Sempione
Go green

DISTANCE: 4km
GRADIENT: Flat
DIFFICULTY: Easy
HIGHLIGHT: The renaissance-era Castello Sforzesco
BEST TIME: Morning or late afternoon
NEAREST METRO STATION: Cairoli

The Parco Sempione makes up for Milan's relative lack of parks. It's not all rolling green like London's Hyde Park or New York's Central Park. Instead, it's a sprawling collection of finely manicured lawns and architectural gems.

Start at the Fontana di Piazza Castello at the foot of the *Castello Sforzesco* – built in the 15th century by Francesco Sforza, the then duke of Milan – and head round the eastern side towards the *Arena Civica Gianni Brera*. This multipurpose stadium hosts rugby matches, music concerts and cultural events and is a beautiful example of early 19th-century neoclassicism.

Continue heading up the park and you'll soon reach the marble *Arco della Pace*. Circle it and head back down the other side of the park towards Gio Ponti's Torre Branca and the neighbouring *Triennale di Milano* – we won't judge if you decide to call it quits here in favour of an exhibition.

At the centre of the park is a small lake; it may be a bit of a roundabout journey to get there from the museum but it's a pleasant leg of the run nonetheless. From there, jog back towards the castle; you can either pass straight through it or work your way around the walls. And remember: although this run is only four kilometres, the Parco Sempione is perfect for laps if you've got energy to spare.

② Centro Storico and Naviglio Grande
Pace yourself

DISTANCE: 8km
GRADIENT: Flat
DIFFICULTY: Easy
HIGHLIGHT: The Colonne di San Lorenzo, Naviglio Grande and historic centre
BEST TIME: Morning
NEAREST METRO STATION: Duomo

This is a fairly long but rewarding run that takes in some of the city's most pleasant streets and major sights. Something to note: don't attempt this course during aperitivo hour or thereafter (17.00 onwards). You'll be stopped in your tracks by a swarm of revellers on the Naviglio Grande and will have no choice but to order a spritz yourself. Of course, maybe that's part of your plan...

Set off outside the *Pinacoteca Ambrosiana*, a gallery established in 1618 by cardinal Federico Borromeo, and head south towards Ticinese, one of the oldest neighbourhoods in Milan. This will take you past the *Colonne di San Lorenzo*, the most important Roman remains in the city.

Once at the Darsena canal port, loop around its western side and proceed down the Naviglio Grande, an artificial canal first developed in the 12th century. It's a long stretch – all the way to the Mediterranean, in fact – but we recommend crossing over and turning back just after the romanesque and gothic *Chiesa di San Cristoforo sul Naviglio*.

Back at the Piazza XXIV Maggio, head along the quaint Via Santa Croce and past the leafy *Parco delle Basiliche*. From here it's a charming and casual jog through the historic centre to the Duomo.

Walks
—— Step up your sightseeing

The most rewarding way to explore Milan is on foot. Despite being the second most populous city in Italy, it's still easy to traverse, often feeling more like a compact renaissance town rather than a major European metropolis. Best of all, the neighbourhoods flow into one another with seamless charm. From bohemian Brera and bourgeois Wagner to gritty Isola and the canals of Ticinese and Navigli, we'll guide you through four fine districts.

NEIGHBOURHOOD 01

Isola
Working-class roots

Taking its name from the Italian word for "island", Isola has always been cut off from the main body of Milan. In fact, it wasn't even considered part of the city until 1873; prior to that it was agricultural land beyond the city walls, known as Corpi Santi. These days it's still somewhat, ahem, isolated from the rest of Milan by rail tracks and Porta Garibaldi station. But it's this separation that has given the area such a strong sense of community.

It was in the early 20th century that Isola began to develop the character for which it has become known. As an industrial heartland where most people were employed to make everything from electrical machinery to soap, it was very much a working-class neighbourhood. Literally on the wrong side of the tracks for many, the district housed the majority of residents in *case di ringhiera (see page 117)* until growth after the Second World War began to bring change. By the 1990s, artists and creatives were moving here for the cheap property and they continue to give Isola a bohemian vibe that's survived the gentrification prompted by the building of the Porta Nuova skyscrapers and plaza.

Today, the area juxtaposes old and new, with leafy streets for outdoor dining, prolific street art and quirky vintage shops to offset the modernisation around Piazza Gae Aulenti.

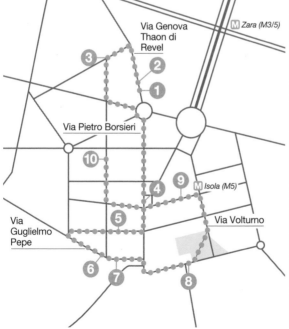

Stroll, snack and sip
Isola walk

Begin with a cappuccino and a croissant in the plant-filled internal courtyard of **1** *Deus Café*. The brunch menu is reason enough to visit but there's plenty more going for this two-level space: you can get your bike fixed at the ground-floor workshop or, if you feel so inclined, stock up on motorbike-related paraphernalia at the shop upstairs.

Once you're fuelled up and ready to go, cross the road to

Getting there

The area has its own metro station, aptly named Isola, which is on the M5 line. Porta Garibaldi station is just a stone's throw away and connected to both the M2 and M5 lines, as well as trains that pull in from outside the city.

2 *Eyeland*. The space may be pint-sized but the choice of spectacles picked by founder Max Brunello is broad and even includes a bespoke, in-house line. Proceed up Via Genova Thaon di Revel until you see the belltower of the church behind the **3** *Teatro Fontana*. A packed programme warrants a visit in the evening if you speak Italian – but even when the curtain's down, ask to see the back cloister: it's a tranquil, frescoed, architectural gem where talks sometimes take place.

Next, head down Via Vincenzo Civerchio and Via Alserio to reach Piazzale Segrino, a small square that hosts a sculptural memorial to anti-Fascist partisans who died during the Second World War. Then proceed down Via Pietro Borsieri, the area's main street. Here you'll find plenty of restaurants worthy of a stop-off but we recommend the outdoor area of **4** *Mo Mo*: the menu is African-inspired (but there's also Brazilian açai and Indian lassi for afters).

Another short hop down Via Pietro Borsieri, past a fascinating

ferramenta (hardware store), will lead you to Via Pastrengo. There are lots of small boutiques nestled on this short stretch: we recommend clothing shop **5** *Rapa*, with items for women, men and children – all designed and made in Italy. Once you get to the end of the street (if you can resist the temptation to park yourself at The Botanical Club for a gin and tonic) turn left and you'll be rewarded with a view of Porta Garibaldi's gleaming skyscrapers.

At the corner with Via Carmagnola, a hideaway awaits: **6** *Libreria Les Mots* has shelves packed with titles by independent publishers but this tiny bookshop also organises language courses and author meet-ups and has a co-working area to boot. Continue down the road to discover the area's peaceful oasis: **7** *Isola Pepe Verde*, a shared garden where residents can tend to vegetables and plants – and visitors can enjoy a seat between the flower beds or join one of the many cultural events that periodically take place.

Circle back to Via Pietro Borsieri and veer right to see the Stefano Boeri-designed **8** *Bosco Verticale* (*see page 104*) then walk between the two towers and through the park to reach Via Volturno. Turn left onto Via Sebenico and head to **9** *Berberè*, a pizzeria that serves one of the best margheritas in town.

Follow Via Sebenico until it becomes Via Jacopo dal Verme and then turn right up Piazzale Carlo Archinto. An ivy-covered courtyard belongs to **10** *Frida* (*see page 44*), a cocktail bar where the negronis are poured until the early hours.

Address book

01 Deus Café
3 Via Genova Thaon di
Revel, 20159
+39 02 8343 9230
deuscustoms.com

02 Eyeland
4 Via Genova Thaon di
Revel, 20159
+39 34 0665 9009
occhialisumisuramilano.it

03 Teatro Fontana
21 Via Gian Antonio
Boltraffio, 20159
+39 02 6901 5733
teatrofontana.it

04 Mo Mo
Piazza Tito Minniti, 20159
+39 02 8708 7480

05 Rapa
5A Via Pastrengo, 20159
+39 02 2316 7868
rapamilano.com

06 Libreria Les Mots
Via Carmagnola and Via
Pepe, 20159
+39 32 8639 2658
librerialesmots.it

07 Isola Pepe Verde
10 Via Pepe, 20159
*isolapepeverde.wordpress.
com*

08 Bosco Verticale
Via Gaetano di Castillia,
20124
stefanoboeriarchitetti.net

09 Berberè
21 Via Sebenico, 20124
+39 02 3670 7820
berberepizza.it

10 Frida
3 Via Antonio Pollaiuolo,
20159
+39 02 680 260
fridaisola.it

NEIGHBOURHOOD O2

Wagner
Slow down and enjoy

When Wagner metro station was unveiled in 1966 and the German composer's surname became the neighbourhood's appellation, the story goes that the more patriotic residents mockingly Italianised the pronunciation to Wanier (like "gn" in gnocchi) and the gag continues today.

One can hardly blame them. Milan has suffered centuries of foreign rule – most notably under the Spanish in the 17th century and the Austrians in the 19th century – so the sentiments of civic pride (or *campanilismo*) sometimes run high. Why was Milan so desired by other European nations? Perhaps for its proximity to the northern border: stand on Wagner's Piazza Michelangelo Buonarroti, look to the northwest and you can make out the ephemeral outline of the Alps. One man who did, and was moved to tears by the sight, was Giuseppe Verdi. The Italian composer's half-smiling, contemplative statue stands in the centre of the piazza. Perhaps he's grinning at the irony of finding himself in a neighbourhood named after a German rival.

A bourgeois district in the 1930s, Wagner is sleepier than Ticinese or Brera, but while its rewards are less obvious, they shouldn't be overlooked. Whether you're after a fine pair of loafers, a bespoke jacket or a delectable meal away from the tourists, Wagner has more to offer than most assume.

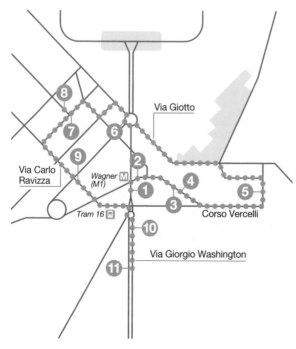

Via Giotto

Via Carlo
Ravizza

Wagner Ⓜ
(M1)

Tram 16 🚏

Corso Vercelli

Via Giorgio Washington

Retail ramble
Wagner walk

Start with a mid-morning coffee and *cornetto* at ❶ *Torrefazione Il Caffè Ambrosiano* – a simple historic café and neighbourhood favourite. Exit right and walk up to Piazza Riccardo Wagner, home to the ❷ *Mercato Comunale Wagner*. The closed market opened in 1929 and is full of fresh produce.

Continue right along the south side of the square as it turns into Via Belfiore. This little shopping

street is home to a few gems, among them ❸ *Belfiore Calzature*, run by the Pontiggia family since 1953. The shoes there span all sorts of styles and won't break the bank, so be sure to grab a pair or two. Further down the road at number 10 is ❹ *Avirex*. The New York label's bomber jackets and chinos were popularised by the likes of Steve McQueen, who wore them in the 1963 film *The Great Escape*. Since the 1980s, the brand has also supplied jackets to the US Air Force.

For something a bit more formal, continue along Via Belfiore; cross the intersecting boulevard and head straight onto Corso Vercelli, one of the neighbourhood's main arteries. The next left brings you to ❺ *Al Bazar*, the home of flamboyant tailor and style icon Lino Ieluzzi. The atelier is stacked with bold-coloured ties, double-breasted jackets and immaculate loafers.

Exit left up the street and then take the first left. On reaching the intersection at the end of Via Giovanni Rasori, cross to

the other side of the opening and walk west along Via del Burchiello with the park on your right. At the next crossroads keep going straight and continue until Piazza Michelangelo Buonarroti. In front of you, you'll see the orange-hued **6** *Casa Verdi*, a retirement home for musicians of merit that was founded in 1899 by the composer himself.

Bid farewell to the old talent and take a left onto Via Monte Rosa, followed by the first left, then first right. Turn left again onto Via Correggio and just up ahead on the corner you'll find mid-century homeware shop **7** *Modernariato de Nicola*. Understandably, you may be feeling rather peckish at this stage, so stop off a little way beyond the shop at top-notch pizza restaurant **8** *Barabba Bistrot*. If, on the other hand, you would like to hold out for a more leisurely meal, continue down Via Correggio.

The next left takes you onto Via Carlo Ravizza. It's lined with shops and restaurants; the place we're after is **9** *Le Lunetier*. The sleek new space offers specs

from the likes of Lindberg and lesser-known names such as Italian talents Epos and Kyme.

Exit right, heading straight to Piazza Piemonte. Turn right past the white Teatro Nazionale and you'll find yourself standing in front of **10** *I Grattacieli*. Though the epithet "skyscrapers" may seem somewhat tongue-in-cheek today, at the time of their building in 1923 these 38-metre twin towers certainly deserved it. Their architect, Mario Borgato, needed to be granted an exemption from a Milanese law that forbade any structure from surpassing 28 metres in height.

Pass between the two, heading down Via Giorgio Washington for the final stop of the walk. On the upcoming right-hand corner is restaurant **11** *Olei*. The speciality here is seafood but pay close attention to the desserts as well: you'll want to get a fork stuck into the Napoleon mille-feuille.

Getting there

The M1 line quickly connects Wagner to Brera, the area around the Duomo, and the up-and-coming Porta Venezia. If you would prefer an old-school alternative, hop on tram number 16 and get off at Piazza Piemonte.

NEIGHBOURHOOD 03
Brera
Art at its heart

Tucked away to the north of the city centre, Brera was once a working-class area popular with the city's artists, creatives and nonconformists. Due to its bohemian past it has gained the moniker "the Milanese Montmartre" and while it may not be as eulogised as its Parisian counterpart – despite its narrow cobbled streets, wrought-iron balconies and façades painted in warm shades of ochre, terracotta and rust – it gives it a run for its money. Better still, it comes without the crowds.

The area was first developed in the 13th century when cloisters were built on meadows beyond the city walls (the name Brera is thought to stem from the medieval Italian *braida* meaning "uncultivated land"). Today it's best known for its design galleries, upscale boutiques and soaring rents but visitors are still likely to encounter the odd fortune teller or tarot-card reader plying their trade from street-side tables draped with cloth. And art remains the beating heart of the neighbourhood thanks to the Palazzo di Brera, which houses one of the city's most important galleries, a fine-art academy, an astronomical observatory and botanical gardens.

This may be one of Milan's most pedestrian-friendly enclaves but beware of those treacherous, ankle-twisting cobblestones: take our advice and slow down the pace a notch.

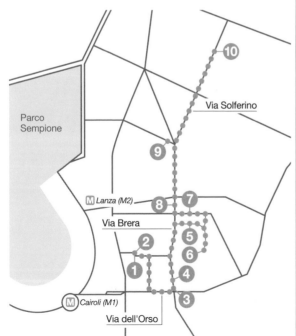

Streetlife sampler
Brera walk

Start in the chic Piazza del Carmine, home to Acne Studios, Aesop and an abstract statue by Polish artist Igor Mitoraj. If the weather is on your side, fuel up with a drink outside **1** *God Save the Food*. The name may be a little inane but the drinks hit the spot and the terrace is perennially popular. Once refreshed, head into the red-bricked **2** *Santa Maria del Carmine* on the edge of the square. Look for the statue of Saint Expeditus on your left as you enter: the patron saint of urgent and desperate causes is depicted brandishing a cross bearing the Latin word *hodie* (today), while crushing a crow croaking *cras* (tomorrow) with his foot. He's particularly popular with Milan's students around exam time.

On exiting, turn left, then left again to take Via del Carmine along the side of the church before turning right onto Via Ciovasso. Walk the length of the cobbled street then turn left onto Via dell'Orso and take the second left onto Via Brera, typically packed with art students and window shoppers. On your right is **3** *Cavalli e Nastri*, with its colourful vintage jewellery and womenswear from the likes of Chanel, Gucci and Hermès. A few doors down is **4** *Pettinaroli*, based in Milan since 1881; pop in and admire its collection of antique globes, maps and stationery.

Carry on along Via Brera until you reach the Palazzo di Brera on your right. The second floor is home to the **5** *Pinacoteca di Brera* (*see page 89*), which hosts one of the most impressive collections of paintings by Italian masters in the world: head here for your fill of Caravaggio, Raphael and Bellini.

Next, make your way back to the main courtyard with its statue of Napoleon and follow the corridor opposite the entrance to the end. Turn right down another corridor and on your left you'll find a door leading to a gravel path. Take this to the right and you'll reach the **6** *Orto Botanico di Brera* (it's not signposted so if you lose

your bearings, just ask). Founded by Maria Theresa of Austria in 1774 and one of the city's true hidden gems, this bucolic pocket of land boasts an impressive range of medicinal herbs, flowers and shrubs laid out in neat strips. Be sure to admire the back of the palazzo: the wisteria-clad turrets and cupolas house Milan's Osservatorio Astronomico.

To exit, rather than heading back into the palazzo continue along the gravel path that runs down the side of the academy until

it joins Via Fiori Oscuri. Turn left and you'll find **7** *Libreria Galleria Demetra* on your right. Owned by book dealer Andrea Oioli, this small bookshop stocks plenty of antiquarian titles from across the past seven centuries.

Turn right out of the shop and at the end of the street veer right back on to Via Brera. Just past the Cesare Crespi art-supply shop you'll find historic bar **8** *Jamaica*. A longtime favourite with the city's art crowd, it was also one of Benito Mussolini's regular haunts (although famously he didn't settle the bill on his last visit).

For some reading material, cross Via Pontaccio and head up Via Solferino to newsstand **9** *Edicola Fabrizio Prestinari* on Largo Claudio Treves; it's open seven days a week. By now, you'll no doubt be ready for some sustenance so head along Via Solferino to **10** *Pisacco*. Another venture by Andrea Berton – the chef behind Dry (*see page 29*) – this smart venue serves inventive, seasonal fare.

Getting there

Piazza del Carmine is within easy reach of both Lanza (M2) and Cairoli (M1) metro stations. It's also a mere 10-minute walk from the Duomo.

Address book

01 God Save the Food
1 Piazza del Carmine, 20121
+39 02 2222 9440
godsavethefood.it

02 Santa Maria del Carmine
2 Piazza del Carmine, 20121
+39 02 8646 3365
chiesadelcarmine.it

03 Cavalli e Nastri
2 Via Brera, 20121
+39 02 7200 0449
cavallienastri.com

04 Pettinaroli
4 Via Brera, 20121
+39 02 8646 4642
fpettinaroli.it

05 Pinacoteca di Brera
28 Via Brera, 20121
+39 02 7226 3264
pinacotecabrera.org

06 Orto Botanico di Brera
28 Via Brera, 20121
+39 02 5031 4696
ortobotanicoitalia.it/ lombardia/brera

07 Libreria Galleria Demetra
3 Via Fiori Oscuri, 20121
+39 02 3674 0699

08 Jamaica
32 Via Brera, 20121
+39 02 876 723
jamaicabar.it

09 Edicola Fabrizio Prestinari
Largo Claudio Treves, 20121
+39 02 659 5290

10 Pisacco
48 Via Solferino, 20121
+39 02 9176 5472
pisacco.it

NEIGHBOURHOOD 04
Ticinese and Navigli
Rich in history

Ticinese and Navigli are often clumped together as one neighbourhood. Ticinese gets its name from Ticinum, the Roman name for nearby town Pavia – to which it's linked by a long road – while Navigli stems from *naviglio*, the Italian word for "canal".

Historically Ticinese was an area of artisans (mainly blacksmiths and tanners), who used the *navigli* for their work. But two world wars gravely marked this densely populated neighbourhood and it soon fell into a state of disrepair.

Leonardo da Vinci and Francesco Sforza were involved in the creation of the *navigli* (*see page 81*). From their initial planning in the 12th century to their final ramification in the 16th century, their purpose was tactical. For more than four centuries they connected Milan to other cities, playing a crucial commercial role and becoming a predominant feature of the city's identity. Although most of the canals were covered up with the advent of the industrial revolution, they have recently been brought back to life and reintegrated into the city.

Today, these two neighbourhoods are the epicentre of *la movida* (nightlife), with plenty of bars and restaurants lining the canals. Come here during the day to appreciate them in a different light: this is when their historical treasures truly shine.

History and art
Ticinese and Navigli walk

Begin your walk at the Parco delle Basiliche, where Via Molino delle Armi meets Piazza Vetra. Follow the path through the park, keeping ❶ *Basilica di San Lorenzo Maggiore* on your left. When the park ends at Via Pio IV, continue down the street to see a series of murals, again on your left. The paintings portray figures who had roles in the city's past such as Napoleon, Giuseppe Verdi, Leonardo da Vinci and Saint Ambrose.

A left turn onto Corso di Porta Ticinese takes you around the front of the basilica to the ❷ *Colonne di San Lorenzo*, 16 columns from Milan's late Roman period. The statue of Emperor Constantine celebrates his Edict of Milan, by which the Empire recognised religious freedom for Christians.

To your right as you look at the statue is a small square. Pop across it and under the arches of what was Porta Cicca, one of the medieval doors through which visitors once entered the city. Cross the street, staying on Corso di Porta Ticinese, and on your right you'll see ❸ *Verso*, a charming bookshop-cum-café that specialises in smaller independent publishing houses. Enjoy a coffee there then continue down the road. After a while you'll reach ❹ *Serendeepity* on your right, the place to go for jazz vinyls, vintage Yves Saint Laurent glasses, books on cinema and photography, and graphic novels.

At the end of the street is Piazza XXIV Maggio, with its monument commissioned by Napoleon to celebrate the Battle of Marengo,

Parco delle Basiliche

Via Vigevano

Bus 94

Tram 3

Via Tortona

Porta **M** Genova (M2)

Alzaia Naviglio Grande

where the French defeated the Austrians on 14 June 1800.

Cross the piazza and turn right towards the redeveloped Darsena, Milan's former turning basin and home to an indoor market and bars. Keep the canal to your right and follow it until you reach Via Vigevano on your left. Less than 100 metres along Via Vigevano is the **5** *Fondazione Arnaldo Pomodoro*; created by the renowned sculptor, the foundation and museum houses more than 50 of his works. At the end of the street is Porta Genova station. Cross the railway tracks via the green footbridge (or the temporary crossing next to it) and go straight ahead down Via Tortona. Turn left onto Via Savona before hanging a right onto Via Montevideo; stop a little way along it for lunch at **6** *PaninoLab*.

Once you're fed, head back the way you came and cross Via Savona to Via Cerano. At the end of the road, bear right on Via Tortona as far as the Largo delle Culture roundabout. Keep right, cross Via Bergognone and enter

number 34. A former steel plant, its big entrance will take you to two different venues: **7** *Base Milano*, a co-working space, bar and set for musical events or film festivals; and **8** *Laboratori Ansaldo*, Teatro alla Scala's backstage fabricators for almost 20 years. This is where every prop is created, from carpentry to background paintings. Make sure you book in advance.

Retrace your steps onto Via Tortona and recross the tracks. Turn right onto Via Valenza, left onto Via Casale and then left again onto Alzaia Naviglio Grande. A short walk takes you to **9** *Vicolo dei Lavandai*, a glimpse of a former wash house used throughout the 1800s by women to do their laundry in the stream.

Retrace your steps to cross the first bridge on your left, turning right along the opposite bank for an aperitivo at **10** *Pinch*. Try one of its signature cocktails with old-school spirits such as Fernet Branca or Zucca. Finally, directly across the *naviglio* is **11** *I Capatosta* should you want to cross over later for one of Milan's best pizzas.

Getting there

Parco delle Basiliche can be easily reached from the Duomo by hopping on tram number 3 to the Colonne di San Lorenzo stop. The 94 bus also serves the park.

Address book

01 Basilica di San Lorenzo Maggiore
35 Corso di Porta Ticinese, 20123
+39 02 8940 4129
sanlorenzomaggiore.com

02 Colonne di San Lorenzo
35 Corso di Porta Ticinese, 20123
+39 02 8940 4129
sanlorenzomaggiore.com

03 Verso
40 Corso di Porta Ticinese, 20123
+39 02 837 5648
libreriaverso.com

04 Serendeepity
100 Corso di Porta Ticinese, 20123
+39 02 8940 0420
serendeepity.net

05 Fondazione Arnaldo Pomodoro
9 Via Vigevano, 20144
+39 02 8907 5394
fondazionearnaldo pomodoro.it

06 PaninoLab
8 Via Montevideo, 20144
+39 02 2222 0034
paninolab.it

07 Base Milano
34 Via Bergognone, 20144
base.milano.it

08 Laboratori Ansaldo
34 Via Bergognone, 20144
+39 02 4335 3521
teatroallascala.org/en/ ansaldo-workshops/ ansaldo.html

09 Vicolo dei Lavandai
14 Alzaia Naviglio Grande, 20144

10 Pinch
63 Ripa di Porta Ticinese, 20143
+39 02 3652 8204

11 I Capatosta
56 Alzaia Naviglio Grande, 20144
+39 02 8941 5910

Resources
⎯⎯ Inside knowledge

By now you should be right up to speed with Milan's boutiques, bars and bistros, have a firm handle on its myriad cultural offerings and know your AC from your Inter. All that's left is to familiarise yourself with the details that will make your trip just that little bit more straightforward.

Here we lift the lid on everything you'll need to get from the airport to the city as well as the best ways to get around once you've arrived. Grab some tips on Milan's dialect, make plans on what to do if the weather is on your side and catch up on the choice events. We'll even throw in some playlist suggestions to get you in the mood.

Transport
Getting around town

01 **On foot:** Central Milan is relatively compact and, thanks to the well-kept streets and orderly traffic (compared to Rome at least), walking is always a viable option. Avoid the busy and uninspiring Via Torino and Corso Buenos Aires, opting for the smaller alleyways and residential streets instead. This way you're more likely to stumble upon an old church, charming shop or other such gem.

02 **Metro:** Milan's metro is efficient, tidy and well-priced, with simple, legible signage designed by Bob Noorda and Franco Albini. There are four metro lines (confusingly numbered 1, 2, 3 and 5 – number 4 is still under construction and due to open in 2022) plus a suburban railway operated by Trenord. Single tickets, valid for 90 minutes, are €1.50 and a 24-hour ticket is €4.50. They're good for both the metro and suburban trains.
atm.it; trenord.it

03 **Taxi:** Taxi drivers tend to be smart and professional. Either call a cab from a company such as Radio Taxi 6969 or hail one on the street. A base tariff is about €5, with roughly €1 for every kilometre thereafter.
026969.it

04 **Bike:** Milan's bike-share scheme, BikeMi, is similar to those found in Paris and London, with more than 4,500 bicycles across town, some of them electric. A day-long fee is €4.50 and allows you to rent the wheels as many times as you desire (in 30-minute windows only, or else there's a surcharge). Milan may be Italy's spiritual cycling homeland (*see page 74*) but beware, those cobbles can make for a bumpy ride.
bikemi.com

Airports
Runway success

01 **Malpensa:** This is Milan's main airport but it's located about 50km to the northwest. The quickest way to and from the city is the Malpensa Express. A return ticket is €20 and trains run every half-hour from Stazione Centrale, Porta Garibaldi and Cadorna, taking between 40 and 50 minutes. A taxi will set you back about €90 and can take more than an hour if the traffic is bad (it often is). There's a taxi rank outside arrivals.
malpensaexpress.it

02 **Linate:** This airport is smaller but significantly closer. The best way to traverse the 7km to central Milan is by taxi but be wary of drivers asking for excessive sums: the average cost is about €20. Bus 73 runs frequently to and from San Babila and takes less than 30 minutes.

Vocabulary
Local lingo

The Milanese dialect – which has a pleasantly rough ring to it and is influenced by German and French – is only regularly spoken among older generations. However, there are a handful of words that are commonly heard on the lips of the city's residents.

01 **Bella!** hey!
02 **Sciura:** an old, fashionable Milanese lady
03 **Zio:** mate or buddy (though it literally means "uncle")
04 **Pirla:** fool
05 **Figo:** cool
06 **Boh:** an interjection used to mean "well", "um" or "I don't know"
07 **Tusa:** girl
08 **Fioeu:** boy
09 **Cornetto:** little croissants typical at breakfast and ubiquitous in cafés
10 **Baùscia:** plucky entrepreneur

Soundtrack to the city
Top tunes

01 Giuseppe Verdi, 'Va, Pensiero' from Nabucco: Exile-themed chorus popular with the Milanese ever since the Italian unification movement in the 19th century.

02 Giorgio Gaber, 'Porta Romana': Gaber's heartfelt take on a 19th-century Milanese ballad.

03 Adriano Celentano, 'Il Ragazzo della Via Gluck': A country boy moves to Milan and years later finds his beloved countryside consumed by the city.

04 Gala, 'Freed from Desire': This single from Gala's debut album took Europe by storm.

05 Baustelle, 'Un Romantico a Milano': Indie rock group Baustelle dedicated this track to journalist, translator and novelist Luciano Bianciardi.

Best events
What to see

01 Fashion Week: Held twice a year. Head to Porta Genova for the dazzling dresses and flamboyant suits; the city streets are the real catwalks. *February/March and September/October, fashionweekonline.com/milan*

02 Giornata Fai di Primavera: For one weekend many of Milan's off-limits palazzos and historical sites are opened to the public by the Fondo Ambiente Italiano. *March, fondoambiente.it*

03 Salone del Mobile: The world's largest furniture fair, held in Rho on the outskirts of town. A plethora of events, parties and installations spring up across the city. *April, salonemilano.it*

04 Milano Food Week: Tastings, workshops and talks take place across town in a week-long celebration of Lombard and Italian cuisine. *May, milanofoodweek.com*

05 Cortili Aperti: The city's grand courtyards open to the public for one Sunday a year. *May, cortiliaperti.it*

06 La Notte Bianca (The White Night): Once a year, bars, restaurants, shops and cinemas stay open all night. *June*

07 Terraforma: Electronic music festival at Villa Arconati. *June-July, terraformafestival.com*

08 Notturni in Villa: Late-night jazz and classical concerts in venues across the city. *June-August, amicidellamusicamilano.it*

09 Milano Film Festival: Independent film festival with screenings citywide. *September-October, milanofilmfestival.it*

10 La Scala opening night: Black tie, red carpet and cocktails are de rigeur. *7 December, teatroallascala.org*

Sunny days
The great outdoors

Summer in Milan can be stifling and most residents escape for the entire month of August, decamping to the mountains, lakes or coast. If you're stuck in the city, head to one of these spots instead.

01 Parco Sempione: Behind the 15th-century Castello Sforzesco (see page 116) is a park with cafés and plenty of shade. If the heat becomes unbearable, take refuge in the Triennale di Milano (see page 92). Otherwise, join the sunbathers by the central lake before dragging yourself to aperitivo at the Piazza Sempione beneath the triumphal arch.

02 Naviglio Grande: Open water in Milan is rare so the Naviglio Grande and the Darsena (the basin at its northernmost point) can get crowded. Thankfully the canal stretches for several kilometres and there's plenty of window-shopping to be done. This is the place to find artists' studios, vintage shops and trendy bars. Finish with a spritz on the waterfront like a true Milanese.

03 Duomo rooftop: Get up close and personal with the saintly statues that adorn the cathedral (there are a record-breaking 3,400 in total). Regular art exhibitions are held on the roof terrace should you tire of the spectacular vista, which extends as far as the Alps on a clear day. Take the elevator for €13 or the stairs for €9. *duomomilano.it*

Rainy days
Weather-proof activities

Unfortunately Milan experiences its fair share of rain – and not the five-minute showers you get elsewhere. If it rains here, it *really* rains. But there's plenty to engage your mind and stomach when the heavens open.

01 Gallerie d'Italia: This gallery occupies a former bank and two palazzos. Deep inside its complex, admiring canvases by Boccioni, you'll forget the deluge outside. It's centrally located too, so it's easy to pop into a café or scurry to another museum or shop. *gallerieditalia.com*

02 Galleria Vittorio Emanuele II: There's no grander shelter than this. Look up to see the water pitter-patter on the glass dome, check out the upscale shops or enjoy a drink at one of the cafés.

03 Get out of town: If it's raining in Milan, maybe the skies are blue over Como? Jump on a train and head north to the lakes or visit renaissance towns such as Piacenza and Bergamo: the area is packed with daytrip options (see page 120).

About Monocle
—— Step inside

In 2007, Monocle was launched as a monthly magazine briefing on global affairs, business, culture, design and much more. We believed there was a globally minded audience of readers who were hungry for opportunities and experiences beyond their national borders.

Today Monocle is a complete media brand with print, audio and online elements – not to mention our expanding network of shops and cafés. Besides our London HQ we have six international bureaux in New York, Toronto, Singapore, Tokyo, Zürich and Hong Kong. We continue to grow and flourish and at our core is the simple belief that there will always be a place for a print brand that is committed to telling fresh stories and sending photographers on assignments. It's also a case of knowing that our success is all down to the readers, advertisers and collaborators who have supported us along the way.

London HQ
Our editorial office is in Marylebone

❶
International bureaux
Boots on the ground

We have an HQ in London and call upon firsthand reports from our contributors in more than 35 cities around the world. We also have six international bureaux. For this travel guide, MONOCLE reporters Joe Pickard, Chiara Rimella, Melkon Charchoglyan and Beatrice Carmi decamped to Milan to explore all that it has to offer. They also called on the assistance of writers in the city, as well as our correspondents Ivan Carvalho and David Plaisant, to ensure that we have covered the best in retail, food, hospitality and entertainment. The aim is to make you, the reader, feel like a local when visiting Milan.

❷
Online
Digital delivery

We have a dynamic website: *monocle.com.* As well as being the place to hear our radio station, Monocle 24, the site presents our films, which are beautifully shot and edited by our in-house team and provide a fresh perspective on our stories. Check out the films celebrating the cities that make up our Travel Guide Series before you explore the rest of the site.

❸
Retail and cafés
Food for thought

Via our shops in Hong Kong, Toronto, New York, Tokyo, London and Singapore we sell products that cater to our readers' tastes and are produced in collaboration with brands we believe in. We also have cafés in Tokyo and London. And if you are in the UK capital visit the Kioskafé in Paddington, which combines good coffee and great reads.